Battles and Skirmishes of the Great Sioux War, 1876–1877

Battles and Skirmishes of the Great Sioux War, 1876–1877

The Military View

Compiled, Edited, and Annotated
by Jerome A. Greene

University of Oklahoma Press : Norman and London

By Jerome A. Greene

Evidence and the Custer Enigma (Kansas City, 1973)
Slim Buttes, 1876: An Episode of the Great Sioux War (Norman, 1982)
Yellowstone Command: Colonel Nelson A. Miles and the Great Sioux War, 1876–1877 (Lincoln, 1991)
Battles and Skirmishes of the Great Sioux War, 1876–1877: The Military View (Norman, 1993)

Library of Congress Cataloging-in-Publication Data

Battles and skirmishes of the Great Sioux War, 1876–1877 : the military view / compiled, edited, and annotated by Jerome A. Greene.
    p.   cm.
    Includes index.
    ISBN 0–8061–2535–7 (alk. paper)
    1. Dakota Indians—Wars, 1876. 2. Cheyenne Indians—Wars, 1876. 3. United States. Army. Cavalry—History. 4. United States. Army. Infantry—History. I. Greene, Jerome A.
    E83.876.B3   1993
    973.8'2—dc20   93–16433
                                            CIP

1   2   3   4   5   6   7   8   9   10

For Linda,
For Being

Contents

Illustrations

Maps

Preface

THE FOLLOWING ESSAYS COMPRISE first-person military
accounts of all principal encounters of the Great Sioux War.
Beyond affording a sense of immediacy, they provide an
important perspective on the events of that conflict, most
notably on the Battle of the Little Big Horn, which over-
shadowed all other military operations in 1876–77. The
selections feature a diverse array of comprehensive participant renderings by members of the army commands
involved, including enlisted men, officers, government
scouts, surgeons, and newsmen who accompanied the
troops. (A subsequent volume will present the Great Sioux
War from the viewpoint of its Indian participants.) Most of
the accounts were prepared soon after the events they
describe; a few consist of recollections penned or given
orally years later and which have been largely forgotten.
The accounts were selected on the basis of their contribu-
tion, clarity, and uniqueness; it is hoped that they will
provide a holistic view of the entire conflict from the viewpoint of its army combatants.

The accounts are products of the times in which they
were written, and their terminology regarding Indians
often reflects that reality; they have not been sanitized in
this book. In all instances, the accounts are preceded by
transitional material necessary for continuity and compre-
hensiveness. Biographical data about each contributor are
included. The accounts have been edited minimally and
only to ensure clarity. By and large, the selections are presented as they originally appeared, and any irrelevant

digressions that have been eliminated are indicated with ellipses. Occasionally, principal officers are referred to by their brevet, or honorary, rank instead of their actual rank, and in those cases actual rank is given in brackets at an officer's first mention. Bracketed material also includes corrections and the insertion of first names and initials if those are omitted in the original document.

Arvada, Colorado   JEROME A. GREENE

Introduction
The Great Sioux War: A Military Perspective
Jerome A. Greene

THIS BOOK CONTAINS PARTICIPANT RENDERINGS of the numerous engagements that composed the Great Sioux War. As the title suggests, most of these engagements can be classified as either battles or skirmishes. By military definition late in the nineteenth century, a "battle" involved the commitment of an entire army, or major forces of it, during an encounter, while a "skirmish" was a smaller engagement involving small parties or detachments from a command. In military parlance, "battles" or "skirmishes" were sometimes generically called "fights," "actions," or "encounters," imprecise definitions that were common during the Indian wars doubtless because of often murky army knowledge about the size and composition of opposing warrior forces.

Such was the nature of the conflict known as the Great Sioux War, a lengthy, disjointed struggle between the U.S. Army and allied tribes of Teton Sioux and Northern Cheyenne Indians that occurred in the span of fifteen months between March 1876 and May 1877. During that period, fifteen armed encounters of varying magnitude and intensity took place in a geographical setting presently encompassed by what is now east-central Wyoming, southeastern Montana, western South Dakota, and northeastern Nebraska, an area of approximately 120,000 square miles.

While thus limited to a few tribes within this broad geographical region, the Great Sioux War nonetheless epitomized the culture conflict that had characterized Indian-white relations for almost four hundred years. For white Americans, it was the largest military undertaking since the close of the Civil War in 1865 and one of the largest campaigns against Indians in American history. For the Indians, the events of 1876–77 came to symbolize the worst elements of the Indian policy of the U.S. government as it applied to their fragile condition as cultural entities.

The war with the Sioux in 1876–77, which involved the Northern Cheyennes from its initial encounter, erupted when the expanding interests of the United States clashed with those of the Teton Lakotas, or western Sioux, in the late 1860s and 1870s. Those Indians had occupied the area of eastern Wyoming, southeastern Montana, and western Dakota and Nebraska for decades. During the Civil War, the Bozeman Trail was opened to the gold fields of western Montana Territory, and troops were sent to protect emigrants along the route. But in 1866, Red Cloud's warriors wiped out Captain William J. Fetterman's command at Fort Philip Kearny, and subsequent engagements proved ineffective in holding the trail. In 1868 the Fort Laramie Treaty created the Great Sioux Reservation in what is now western South Dakota and permitted the Sioux and their allies to hunt the region west to the Big Horn Mountains and north to the Powder River country.

Violations of the treaty became common after 1874, when an expedition to the Black Hills in western Dakota found gold in paying quantities. The army tried to stem the resulting rush into the hills by whites, but gave up when the politicians decided to force the issue with several thousand "Northern Sioux" led by Sitting Bull and others who had spurned all efforts to settle them on the reserve. Accordingly, the commissioner of Indian affairs ordered these tribesmen onto the reservation. They did not—or could not—respond promptly, and early in 1876 the situation was turned over to the War Department for resolution.

Generals William T. Sherman and Philip H. Sheridan were the senior officers responsible for initiating and directing military campaigns against the Sioux. With Commanding General Sherman's approval, Missouri Division Commander Sheridan formulated a winter maneuver to strike the Indians—now officially termed "hostiles"—while they were immobilized with weakened ponies in stationary camps. Sheridan ordered Brigadier General George Crook to lead an army north from Fort Fetterman, Wyoming Territory, to attack Sioux known to be wintering along frozen streams in the Powder River region.

On March 17, a contingent of almost four hundred soldiers from Crook's command under Colonel Joseph J. Reynolds fell on a snowy village along the Powder River, driving out the occupants and capturing a large pony herd. But the warriors returned and fought back vigorously, eventually retrieving their ponies and delivering Reynolds—and Crook—a strategic loss. Reynolds had ordered the village contents destroyed, whereas Crook had planned to continue his campaign rationed by stores from the village. Reynolds suffered losses of four men killed and six wounded. Indian casualties apparently totaled one killed and one wounded. Perhaps more significant in the long run, the village had contained not Sioux but Northern Cheyennes, and the Battle of Powder River effectively tightened the Teton-Cheyenne alliance for mutual security. Frustrated by Reynolds's performance, Crook had no choice but to withdraw his cold and hungry soldiers from the field, his campaign a failure.

Almost three months after the Reynolds fight on Powder River, Crook struck north from Fort Fetterman again. This time he led a thousand men. His command comprised one of three military columns in a grand strategy conceived by Sheridan. The other columns were commanded by Colonel John Gibbon and Brigadier General Alfred H. Terry. Gibbon's column moved east down the Yellowstone

River from Fort Shaw, Montana, while Terry's moved west from Fort Abraham Lincoln, Dakota. The three columns were to converge on the Powder River–Yellowstone region, where Sitting Bull, Crazy Horse, and the other nontreaty Sioux roamed.

Crook's force opened contact with the Indians in a brief skirmish on June 9 along the upper reaches of Tongue River. Eight days later, his men awoke to face a phenomenon: Sioux and Cheyenne warriors initiating an attack on their bivouac along the headwaters of Rosebud Creek in Montana. A day-long battle raged that pitted Tetons against not only the army but also its Crow and Shoshone allies. By day's end Crook still held his ground, but any offensive he hoped to maintain had collapsed. Sustaining casualties of ten men killed and twenty-one wounded, Crook turned his soldiers south, marched to Goose Creek in northern Wyoming to await supplies and reinforcements, and effectually withdrew from the campaign. At the Rosebud, where Indian losses numbered about eleven killed and five wounded, the warriors had bested Crook and—although they did not know it at the time—had laid the groundwork for their greatest victory, one that made the army's campaign fizzle over the next three months.

Scarcely one week after the Rosebud encounter came that of the Little Big Horn. Believing that Crook was still moving north, and assured that the concentration of Indians occupied Little Big Horn Valley, General Terry directed Lieutenant Colonel George A. Custer to move with his Seventh Cavalry up the Rosebud after those Indians. Custer ascended the stream, found a huge trail, and headed west. On the morning of June 25, Custer's Crow and Arikara scouts sighted a village on the Little Big Horn. Rather than surround the encampment and attack at dawn, as was standard army practice, Custer determined to execute the tactic at midday—with historic results. The Battle of the Little Big Horn, which lasted several hours, sent

Custer and more than 260 cavalrymen to their deaths at the hands of a native coalition headed by such leaders as Crow King, Gall, Low Dog, Two Moon, and Lame White Man in addition to the prominent duo of Sitting Bull and Crazy Horse. Indian losses at Little Big Horn probably totaled fewer than one hundred killed and wounded.

The Little Big Horn victory created an exuberance among the tribesmen that many recognized as fleeting, for in the loss of Custer and his men lay the seeds of reprisal and inevitable defeat of the victors. Congress and the army reacted quickly, and reinforcements for the stricken commands reached the field within weeks. Crook, Terry, and Gibbon were left to prosecute the war to conclusion and to exact as swift and fitting a retribution as could be attained. Yet the objective was not easily attained, for their commands remained disheartened over repeated losses now punctuated with a catastrophe almost beyond belief. In time, the Custer battle transcended all else in the public mind. Today it represents the essence of not only the Great Sioux War but the entire span of the Indian wars as well.

For several weeks after the Battle of the Little Big Horn, the Sioux campaign—from the army's point of view—stood in danger of foundering. Field administration was in disarray as the troops of Terry and Crook awaited orders. Reinforcements rushed to the front as soon as possible while the Indians moved away and began to break into smaller groups. In early July a scouting party from Crook's command had a near-fatal run-in with one of those groups, and on July 17, in the first major confrontation since the Custer fight, Colonel Wesley Merritt's Fifth Cavalry, en route to join Crook, engaged a large force of Cheyennes in northwestern Nebraska who were headed into the war zone to support Sitting Bull and Crazy Horse. In a brief skirmish that left one warrior dead, Merritt forced the tribesmen back to the Red Cloud Agency.

Finally, in early August, Crook moved north from

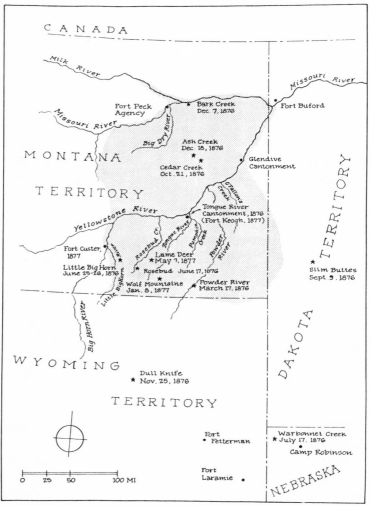

Area of the Great Sioux War, 1876–1877, showing principal zone of activity and locations of major battles and skirmishes.

Goose Creek with twenty-two hundred men plus a body of Crow and Shoshone scouts. Under orders to unite with General Terry, Crook advanced down the Rosebud and on August 10 encountered Terry's force. The two commands marched together until August 25, when Crook set his own course and headed east while Terry and Gibbon withdrew their exhausted soldiers from the field.

Crook's infantry and cavalry trailed the Indians to the Little Missouri River, where his scouts had a brush with the rear guard of one of the Sioux villages. By early September, his men low on rations and his horses starving, Crook ordered the mounts shot and butchered for food. His destination was the Black Hills, where warriors returning to the Nebraska agencies threatened the mining settlements.

Hoping to obtain provisions for his command, Crook on September 7 mounted a party of 150 men under Captain Anson Mills and sent it toward the Black Hills, almost 150 miles to the south. Two days later, Mills's men came upon a village of thirty-seven lodges at Slim Buttes, in what is now the northwestern corner of South Dakota. Mills struck at dawn, driving out men, women, and children and capturing a large pony herd. Most of the Indians fled the Slim Buttes village to seek refuge in Crazy Horse's camp several miles away. By the time Crook came up with the rest of the command, Mills had secured the area. A number of Indians had sought shelter in an adjacent ravine. Crook's soldiers sent hundreds of bullets into the defile before the few occupants, including Chief American Horse, surrendered. Late in the afternoon warriors from Crazy Horse's village attacked the troops, who managed to drive them off. The contents of the tepees went to sustain the famished soldiers.

Crook's casualties numbered three men killed and twenty-four wounded; Indian losses apparently numbered about ten killed and two wounded. Slim Buttes, which constituted the first army victory of the Sioux War, occurred some six months after the warfare had begun. Following Slim Buttes, Crook led his men through the Black Hills to Camp Robinson, Nebraska, where his summer campaign ended.

Prosecution of the war did not conclude with Crook's withdrawal from the field. In the fall, Sitting Bull and his followers moved north of the Yellowstone River to hunt buffalo. Meanwhile, General Sheridan's grand strategy envisioned establishment of a permanent military presence along the Yellowstone. To that end, Terry had left Colonel Nelson A. Miles with units of the Fifth and Twenty-second infantry regiments to occupy an upriver post through the winter. Miles raised a cantonment where the Tongue River entered the Yellowstone and patrolled the wilderness on both sides of the Yellowstone to ensure that the Indians north of that stream did not reunite with those south of it.

A young officer of resource, imagination, and ability, Miles relished his assignment. While construction of the cantonment proceeded, he initiated large-scale campaigning against the Sioux. During mid-October, a wagon train bound for the new post was attacked by Sitting Bull's warriors near Spring Creek, along the north side of the Yellowstone. The Hunkpapa leader sent a message to Miles and his men ordering them out of the buffalo grounds. On October 20, Miles arranged for a council with Sitting Bull—the first face-to-face meeting of any federal agent with the warring Indian leadership since the inception of the conflict. During the exchange, Sitting Bull reiterated his position that the soldiers must leave the region, a notion that Miles rejected. Bereft of food and clothing, many of the tribesmen were becoming destitute as the season grew colder. Noting that some of the Indians showed an inclination to yield, Miles demanded Sitting Bull's surrender but did not get it.

After again failing to reach accord in a meeting the

next day near Cedar Creek, Miles ordered his infantrymen to attack Sitting Bull's position on the surrounding hills. The fight was a wide-ranging affair in which the warriors ignited the prairie and forced Miles's soldiers to pursue them through flames and smoke. Yet while Miles sustained only a few men wounded, Sitting Bull lost five warriors killed in the action. The troops chased the Indians to the Yellowstone, and on October 27 several hundred—minus Sitting Bull—surrendered to Miles and agreed to go into the agencies. The Hunkpapa leader fled north with his immediate followers.

Miles went after Sitting Bull in early November. Leaving the cantonment in charge of men of the Twenty-second Infantry, he moved north with 450 men of the Fifth Infantry and passed up Big Dry River to Fort Peck, a trading post on the Missouri River. Responding to reports that Sitting Bull had gone west, Miles led his men through snow and freezing temperatures but failed to find the Sioux. Early in December, he detached a battalion of three companies under command of Lieutenant Frank D. Baldwin to return to Fort Peck and follow Sitting Bull east. Baldwin's men skirmished with the tribesmen on December 7 on the frozen Missouri River near the mouth of Bark Creek, and eleven days later he surprised Sitting Bull's camp along Ash Creek south of the Missouri. Attacking at dawn, Baldwin's men destroyed the tribesmen's homes and drove them into the cold. Following Miles's Fort Peck expedition, and particularly Baldwin's fight on December 18, Sitting Bull, who eventually crossed into Canada, ceased to be a major factor in the war.

While Miles was maneuvering north of the Yellowstone, events transpired far to the south that largely ended Northern Cheyenne participation in the war. General Crook had undertaken another expedition that included Colonel Ranald S. Mackenzie and his Fourth Cavalry regiment plus elements of the Second, Third, and Fifth cavalry regiments and a contingent of Indian scouts. On November 25, Mackenzie's men struck a large village of Northern Cheyennes under Dull Knife and Little Wolf in a canyon of the Red Fork of Powder River in east-central Wyoming. The attack killed at least forty Indian men and sent refugees fleeing into subzero temperatures that many did not survive. Army casualties in this complete victory for the troops numbered six killed and twenty-five wounded. Mackenzie's fight with Dull Knife's people was one of the largest engagements of the war and was of major consequence in ending it. Distraught Indian men, women, and children, many of them wounded, struggled through snowdrifts and subzero nighttime temperatures to find succor in Montana among Crazy Horse's Oglalas.

Following his return from the Fort Peck expedition, Miles turned his attention south to those Indians wintering along the headwaters of the Rosebud and Tongue. This assemblage included several Teton subtribes, but notably the Oglalas of Crazy Horse and the Northern Cheyennes, including those from Dull Knife's destroyed village. When raiding by warriors associated with these camps increased in the area of the cantonment, Miles determined to move on them at once. Leaving the mouth of the Tongue in late December, the troops of the Fifth and Twenty-second infantry regiments ascended that stream garbed in heavy buffalo overcoats and sealskin caps. On January 7, Miles's scouts captured several Indian women. Next morning, as the command prepared breakfast along the Tongue, Crazy Horse and his warriors attacked from the surrounding hills. Miles responded with a bold offense, his soldiers advancing on all segments of the line, the men scaling the icy heights in a raging blizzard to counter the Indians. Artillery barrages eventually dissuaded the attackers, and when a prominent Cheyenne medicine man named Big Crow fell mortally wounded, the assault collapsed. Miles's losses at Wolf Mountains stood at one man killed and nine wounded. The Indians lost about three killed and the same number wounded. Over the next few days the soldiers trudged back down the Tongue to the cantonment.

The Wolf Mountains battle was followed in February and March by several peace initiatives alternately arranged by Miles and Crook. Many of the Indians, among them Crazy Horse, journeyed to the agencies to turn themselves in; several hundred others, mostly Cheyennes, surrendered to Miles at Tongue River. For all practical purposes, the Sioux War was over.

A few Indians still refused to surrender, however. One small band led by the Minneconjou chief Lame Deer returned to the upper Rosebud country committed to hold out and to defy Miles. Early in May, Miles again led his troops south. They consisted of 450 men of the Fifth and Twenty-second infantry regiments augmented by a four-company battalion of the Second Cavalry. At daylight on May 7, approaching Lame Deer's village of sixty-one lodges along Muddy Creek, Miles sent his cavalrymen to charge through the camp and capture the ponies while his infantrymen fired into the tepees, driving the tribesmen into hills west of the stream. Soon after, the soldiers sacked and burned the village, and next day they marched for the cantonment. Army losses at Muddy Creek were four dead and nine wounded, while the Indians suffered fourteen of their people killed and an unknown number wounded. Over the next few months, the refugees from Lame Deer's village fled east, where most surrendered at the agencies.

From a military standpoint, Miles's persistent campaigning closed the Sioux War. Official records, prominently reflecting the Custer debacle, account for 408 army casualties in the fighting of 1876–77: 283 officers and men (including Indian scouts) killed and 125 wounded. Indian losses for the duration of the conflict are harder to ascertain, but a reasonable figure based upon the testimony of warrior participants places them at approximately 150 killed and 90 wounded in combat. Noncombatant losses are unknown, but were probably high. For the Indians, the opening salvoes of the Great Sioux War were theirs. Rosebud and Little Big Horn marked their military zenith, but Slim Buttes, the Dull Knife Battle, Wolf Mountains, and the Lame Deer Fight signaled their nadir. Forced by necessity to abandon their early summer unity for grass and game, their ultimate fragmentation and near destitution ended all hopes of maintaining their unfettered existence. In this respect, for the Indians who fought Custer, Crook, and Miles, Little Big Horn was the beginning of the end, for it ushered in the crisis of the reservation experience—an experience that lingers to this day.

Sources

Gray, John S. *Centennial Campaign: The Sioux War of 1876.* Fort Collins, Colo.: Old Army Press, 1976.

Greene, Jerome A. *Slim Buttes, 1876: An Episode of the Great Sioux War.* Norman: University of Oklahoma Press, 1982.

———.*Yellowstone Command: Colonel Nelson A. Miles and the Great Sioux War, 1876–77.* Lincoln: University of Nebraska Press, 1991.

Hedren, Paul L. *First Scalp for Custer: The Skirmish at Warbonnet Creek, Nebraska, July 17, 1876.* Glendale, Calif.: The Arthur H. Clark Company, 1980.

———. *Fort Laramie in 1876: Chronicle of a Frontier Post at War.* Lincoln: University of Nebraska Press, 1988.

Hutton, Paul A. *Phil Sheridan and His Army.* Lincoln: University of Nebraska Press, 1985.

Mangum, Neil C. *Battle of the Rosebud: Prelude to the Little Bighorn.* El Segundo, Calif.: Upton and Sons, 1987.

Record of Engagements with Hostile Indians within the Division of the Missouri, from 1868 to 1882, Lieutenant-General P. H. Sheridan, Commanding. Washington, D.C.: Government Printing Office; reprint, Bellevue, Nebr.: Old Army Press, 1969.

"Statement of Casualties among rank and file, United States Army, during the late war with Sioux Indians, commencing in February 1876." Adjutant General's Office, December

11, 1877. Record Group 92, Records of the Office of the Quartermaster General, National Archives.

Stewart, Edgar I. *Custer's Luck*. Norman: University of Oklahoma Press, 1955.

Utley, Robert M. *Frontier Regulars: The United States Army and the Indian, 1866–1891*. New York: The Macmillan Company, 1973.

Vaughn, Jesse W. *The Reynolds Campaign on Powder River*. Norman: University of Oklahoma Press, 1961.

——. *With Crook at the Rosebud*. Harrisburg, Pa. The Stackpole Company, 1956.

Vestal, Stanley. *New Sources of Indian History, 1850–1891*. Norman: University of Oklahoma Press, 1934.

Webb, George W. *Chronological List of Engagements between the Regular Army of the United States and Various Tribes of Hostile Indians Which Occurred during the Years 1790 to 1898, Inclusive*. Saint Joseph, Mo.: Wing Printing Company, 1939; reprint, New York: AMS Press, 1976.

Battles and Skirmishes of
the Great Sioux War,
1876–1877

Chapter 1
The Battle of Powder River, March 17, 1876
Robert E. Strahorn

*When Brigadier General George Crook's army embarked north
from Fort Fetterman, Wyoming Territory, on March 1, 1876, its
movement precipitated the first major combat of the Great Sioux
War. With Crook's command rode Colonel Joseph J. Reynolds,
whose long army career included service in the Mexican and
Civil wars and whose involvement in the campaign against the
Indians would terminate his career in discord and controversy
following the Battle of Powder River on March 17 in southeastern Montana Territory.*

*Newspaperman Robert E. Strahorn, representing the
Rocky Mountain News as well as papers in Chicago, New York,
Omaha, and Cheyenne, accompanied the Crook-Reynolds column. The twenty-four-year-old Pennsylvanian had gained extensive experience as a writer and printer in Illinois and Colorado before joining the News staff in 1871. Through a friendship
with one of Crook's officers, Strahorn was invited to join the
expedition in time for the Powder River movement; he stayed
with Crook throughout the balance of the Sioux conflict and
often rode into battle with the troops, as he did at Powder River,
thereby affording himself a unique perspective and giving his
news accounts an immediate and personal tone. Following Powder River, Strahorn received a War Department commendation
for gallantry for his combat service.*

*After the Sioux War, Strahorn remained in the West. He
wrote a successful guidebook about Wyoming Territory that in-
spired financier Jay Gould to hire him as a publicist for westward migration. Strahorn developed into a serious student of the
West while gathering data to facilitate railroad promotion and
settlement. Ultimately he assumed a leadership role in various
enterprises related to railroading and emigration, and settled in
Spokane, where he headed a number of regional railroads and
utility companies. Strahorn died in 1944, the last of the several*

3

Newspaper correspondent Robert E. Strahorn, who accompanied Crook's column during the Sioux War. Courtesy of the Idaho State Historical Society, No. 978.

*news correspondents with Crook in 1876. His account of the
Battle of Powder River appeared in the* Rocky Mountain News
on April 7, 1876.

WITHOUT DOUBT THE MOST REMARKABLE EVENT of General Crook's present campaign was the night march commenced early on the evening of the 16th inst. As a matter of history it well deserves a place by the side of any similar incident known to frontier service; and if the three hundred gallant and uncomplaining spirits who participated in its thrilling scenes had nothing more whereof to tell in future bivouacs around more peaceful fires, this would be enough. A hard day's march had just been accomplished; man and beast had earned the hardy fare, and the bed of frozen ground that usually were their lot; but the circumstance narrated in my last changed the aspect of affairs. A leader like General Crook was in search of just such circumstances, and if there were any complaints heard in connection with the swiftness of his movements, they came from those whose lot it was to remain behind. Therefore, in about two hours after reaching Otter Creek, with darkness already shadowing the gulches, the two squadrons pushed swiftly and silently forward. A cutting breeze, with its usual perversity in these parts, drove the falling snow directly in our faces. The storm, with not even a moonlit sky above, served to deepen the gloom so rapidly that we were little more than out of sight of the camp-fires left behind until the blackest of nights was upon us. Riding at the head of the scouts, in company with Colonel [Major Thaddeus H.] Stanton and Lieutenant J. G. Bourke—the latter aid-de-camp to General Crook—I had, during the night, an excellent opportunity of witnessing the truly remarkable achievement of Frank Gruard [Grouard], our principal guide and trailer. His knowledge of the country had been noteworthy ever since the opening of the campaign, but the duty he was now called upon to perform was of just the nature that would have bewildered almost any one in broad daylight. He had orders to follow the "back trail" of the two Indians we had seen early in the evening, lead where it would. This he did through the entire night, in the face of a storm that was constantly rendering the pony track of the two savages less distinct, while it was also hourly increasing the tedium of travel. Over rugged bluffs, up narrow valleys, through gloomy defiles and down break-neck declivities, plunged the indomitable Frank; now down on his hands and knees in the deep snow, scrutinizing the faint foot-prints, then, losing the trail for an instant, darting to and fro until it was found, and again following it up with the keenness of a hound, and a fearlessness that would have imbued almost any one with fresh vim and courage. Nor should we forget his valuable assistants, Baptiste Gagnier [Garnier], Jack Russell, Baptiste Poirrier [Pourier], Louis Gingras and others of our keen-eyed scouts, who were practically indispensable. With such unfailing celerity was this trailing accomplished that during almost every hour of the long night orders would come from the rear to halt in order that the command might be kept "closed up."

Toward morning the clouds commenced breaking, and soon the sky was almost clear. But with the change came the most intense cold we had ever experienced, and were it not that the almost exhausted men were compelled to walk and lead their horses much of the way, on account of the roughness of the country, many cases of freezing must have been recorded. And the worst was yet to come. At four in the morning we halted upon what seemed the apex of this entire region. We had at least been ascending quite rapidly nearly all night, and now, by the aid of the dim starlight, and through the thick, frosty atmosphere, we could look down, down, as far as the strained vision would reach, into a wilderness of mountain, forest and vale. How to get down, and at the same time be morally certain of striking the Indians at once, was then the question—for we knew that somewhere through that mass of rocky upheavals must flow the Powder. Again the ever-ready scouts were to show us their true worth, and, with Frank in the lead, off they bounded to find or make a way. Near the summit upon which we had thus briefly halted was a deep, narrow ravine, and in order to have his men as well sheltered as possible while waiting, General [Colonel] Reynolds ordered the command to take position therein and dismount. Here a scene was presented which we can never forget. The cold grew in intensity, and exert ourselves as we would to keep up a circulation, it seemed almost unendurable. The fatiguing marches of the day and night, the great strain upon the nerves caused by the loss of sleep and the continuous cold, the hunger, too, making itself felt, and our not being permitted to enkindle a single fire, however small, on account of the danger of alarming the foe—all of these influences combined told severely upon the strongest physiques. Making my way up and down the gulch in which the shivering men and horses were crowded like bees in a hive, I had no trouble in discovering how they were bearing up under such difficulties. There were very few complaints, but every few moments some poor fellow would drop into the snow, "just for a minute, you know," and when at once shaken up by his more determined comrades, would make all sorts of excuses to be allowed to enter that sleep which, if undisturbed, would have known no waking. Officers were everywhere on the alert to keep their men upon their feet, and, thanks to this general watchfulness, no cases of amputation are yet known to be necessary on account of freezing, although nearly all of us are now nursing frost-bitten feet, faces, or ears. At daylight the returning scouts reported the discovery of a trail leading down to the river, and that the stream was yet some three or four miles distant. An advance was at once ordered—an order that was obeyed with more than usual willingness.

In less than an hour the scouts, who had again been pushed far in advance, came back with the pleasing intelligence that the encampment of Crazy Horse, consisting of over a hundred lodges, lay under the shelter of the mountain we were then descending. They described its situation as best they could and advised that in making the attack the command separate, as two gulches leading down into the valley admitted of an approach from two directions. A short consultation was held which resulted in plans for an immediate attack, General Reynolds detailing the Egan Greys, Company K, Second Cavalry, Captain James Egan, to charge through the village from the upper end, to, if possible, thoroughly demoralize the foe from the start and drive him out of the brush; Companies F, Third, and E, Second Cavalry, Captain [Alexander] Moore, battalion commander, and Lieutenant W. W. Rawolle, to dismount, take a position on the left of the village and thus prevent the escape of the savages; Company I, Second Cavalry, Captain H. E. Noyes, to cut out the ponies and drive them from the field; and Companies M and E, Third Cavalry, Captain A. Mills and Lieutenant J. B. Johnson, to act as reserve. These preliminaries being arranged and a thorough understanding arrived at by the various officers, they at once proceeded toward the positions assigned, each headed by about an equal number of the fifteen or twenty scouts. Colonel Stanton, having virtually finished his duties as chief of scouts by piloting the command to the camp of the foe, could have consistently remained at headquarters, but, dismounting, shouldering his long rifle and advancing at the head of Captain Moore's column, it was quite evident that he didn't propose to stop until the fight ended, at least. Lieutenant Bourke, also detached from any command, and myself cast our fortunes with Captain Egan, by whose side we remained during the continuance of the fight.

Colonel Joseph J. Reynolds, Third U.S. Cavalry, who
commanded the assault on the Northern Cheyennes at
Powder River. Reynolds is shown in the Civil War uni-
form of a major general. Courtesy of Paul L. Hedren.

Separating a mile or more from the village, both divisions had an extremely serious time of it getting over the ground—more especially the one with which we were connected, because we were compelled to take our horses while the others left theirs behind under a suitable guard. The Indians had good reason to wonder at the idea of a command of cavalry coming from that direction, considering the terrific plunges our horses were compelled to make down icy canons, through fallen timber and over dangerous rock-strewn chasms. However, Captain Egan does not believe in impossibilities, and in less than thirty minutes we had floundered to the bottom. Here, securely hid by a low bluff, we could look over and see the village spread out in full view, yet nearly a mile distant. Its position was such as a more civilized chieftain might have selected, and crafty Crazy-Horse rose considerably in our estimation as with one long, eager look we took in those points which particularly interested us now—its adaptability for speedy abandonment rather than its strength. Looking down the valley, between us and the camp, lay a long, wide stretch of bench land, a natural pasturage; meeting this, and with an elevation from ten to twelve feet lower, was a narrow belt of bottom land, with the river washing it on the right. At the limit of this view, where the river swept quite closely around the base of a high and very rugged mountain, and on our side of the stream, lay the object of so much toil and search. The hundred and odd tepees were nestled quite cosily in a grove of large cottonwoods, and on the lower and river side were sheltered by a dense growth of willows. Scattered here and there, quietly feeding along both banks of the stream, were bands of hundreds of ponies.

Not the slightest mistrust or alarm was apparent in this forest home, and it was undoubtedly as clear a case of surprise as there is on record. Arms were hastily inspected, belts filled with cartridges, overcoats and other impediments to ease of movement strapped to the saddles, and, after a thorough inspection of the ground lying between us and the village to aid an undiscovered approach, the eager little squad was ordered to creep forward to cover, a little further on, before mounting. That point reached, a few brief instructions were given by Captain Egan to the effect that the horses should be trotted slowly over the ground until it was certain that we were discovered, then, drawing our revolvers, we should put the steeds to the full gallop, dash into the village with as much force, and with as terrific yells as possible, and when once among the savages to empty our six-shooters "where they would to the most good." Obtaining cover by winding down around the back of the bench-land referred to, and securing good ground on the edge of the river bottom, the order to "fall in for charge" was soon given by the clear-headed captain. In a twinkling the company, with only half its complement of men, swung beautifully forward with one solid front for the charge.

Revolvers were drawn with a grip that meant something more than parade, the pace was slightly accelerated, and, when within less than two hundred yards of the nearest tepee, the first terror-stricken savage was seen to run and loudly whoop the alarm. "*Charge, my boys!*" came like an electric flash from the dauntless leader, and, giving their magnificent gray steeds rein and spur, and yelling like so many demons, the gallant "forty-seven" bounded into the village with the speed and force of a hurricane. With the savages swarming out of their tepees and scattering almost under our feet, we fired right and left at their retreating forms, our horses meanwhile worked into such a frenzy by the din of whoops and yells and discharging arms that they fairly flew over the ground. The demoralization of the foe seemed to last but an instant. A majority of the redskins snatched their arms as they ran, dropped as though shot, behind a log or stump, in the tall grass, or took temporary

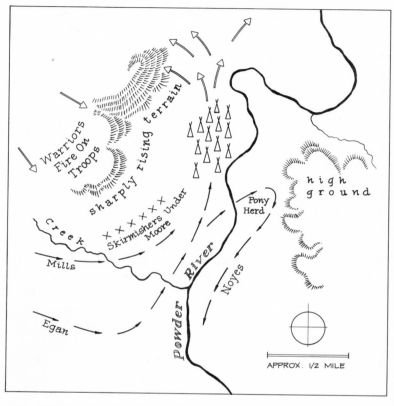

The Battle of Powder River, March 17, 1876.

refuge in the thickets of willow and plum. Bullets and casualties were then bestowed upon us with a will that showed plainly we were not to sweep the field without paying a penalty. The beautiful gray horses were a splendid mark for the Indians, and four or five dropped before we got through the village, Captain Egan's own animal being among the number. Then, with the desperate foe pouring in bullets from behind every convenient cover in the shape of rocks, trees, thickets, etc., we were ordered to dismount, turn our horses over to every fourth man, and continue the fight with our carbines. Our position was now indeed a critical one. In vain did we scan the faces and foot of the bluffs which Captain Moore was ordered to occupy. No troops were in sight, and the savages, evidently believing no other force at hand, must have thought it an easy matter to annihilate us in a very short course of events. But Captain Egan did not seem to think the case quite so desperate and soon ordered a charge through the brush on foot. While advancing, the savages resisting at every step, a small detachment of troops was seen coming down the hill to the left of where we had looked for the command of Captain Moore, but instead of that officer we afterward learned that it was Colonel Stanton, who, finding that Captain Moore was not endeavoring to get into position, secured half a dozen men and advanced to the scene of action. Soon after Captain Mills and Lieutenant Johnson, with companies M and E, 3rd cavalry, came forward and did excellent service in assisting to drive the enemy from the field and in destroying the village. I am informed that Captain Moore also finally followed in the wake of Captain Mills, after the Indians had taken advantage of the loop hole left in their rear and escaped.

The Indians, severely punished, and driven from their village, took refuge in the mountain thus unguarded, and from that time forward, aside from the destruction of their property, had a positive advantage over the troops. Scattered all over this almost impregnable mountain-side, and secreted behind its numerous walls of rock, they could pick off our men without running the slightest risk of losing their own lives. Therefore the more the engagement was prolonged after the prime object of the expedition was accomplished, the more serious and useless were our losses. Realizing this, General Reynolds, at 2 P.M., after a five hours' engagement, ordered the command to abandon its position and to at once proceed toward the mouth of Lodge Pole—the rendezvous appointed by General Crook—

some twelve miles up the river, which point was reached at dark.

With all the scenes of native splendor and luxury our fancy had pictured, this Powder river reality yet excels, yet astonishes. In the more than one hundred large tepees totally destroyed were beds of furs and robes that, to a soldier, looked simply fit for savage gods; war bonnets and squaw dresses, regal in their construction and decoration, requiring months for making, and worth from five to ten ponies each; cooking utensils that an ordinary housewife would not need be ashamed of; tons of dried and fresh meats, and occasionally dried fruits; every tepee an arsenal within itself, with its kegs and canisters of powder; its large supply of bar lead, caps and fixed ammunition; and then piles of such miscellaneous articles as axes, knives, saddles—over 125 of these—buckskin clothing of every description, moccasins, beautifully ornamented saddlebags, sewing outfits, and really everything any frontiersman would need to insure his comfort. With the exception of a few robes and other trinkets removed by the troops, these vast stores, in many instances the accumulation of a lifetime, were piled upon the dismantled tepees and the whole reduced to ashes. In the case of the generous piles of nicely dried meat this action was particularly unfortunate, as the troops needed such provender badly, and General Crook had especially impressed upon the minds of the officers the importance of saving it.

But the grand item in this connection was the capture of a herd of 700 ponies, horses and mules, many of which were of the best class, and identified as belonging to various stock men on the Colorado and Wyoming frontier. These were gathered and driven a short distance from the battle field by the command of Captain Noyes, assisted by the scouts. However, this triumph was of comparatively short duration, as a few of the never-sleeping Indians swooped down upon the herd this morning, and recaptured nearly the entire band. Leaving no orders for the disposal of the ponies yesterday on the field, General Reynolds also neglected to place a guard around them last night, when Colonel Stanton—who, with a few scouts, had taken it upon himself to drive them twenty miles to their camp—turned them over to him. Also, when at daylight, this morning, the ponies were reported as being driven off by the Indians, the general declined sending a force in pursuit, although they could easily have been recovered.

The loss of the savages in killed and wounded cannot even be approximated, although men who were on the skirmish line during the engagement state it all the way from thirty to fifty. Retreating slowly, as they did after our first onslaught, and nearly always close to cover of some kind, they had no difficulty in removing every body from one position to another.

The command suffered a loss of four killed and five wounded. The killed were private Peter Dowdy, Co. E, Third cavalry; Michael McCannon, Co. I, Second cavalry; Lorenzo E. Ayers, Co. M, Third cavalry; George Schneider, Co. K, Second cavalry. Wounded: Patrick Goings, artificer, Co. K, Second cavalry, seriously; Edward Egan, private same company, seriously; John Lang, corporal, Co. E. Second cavalry, slightly; Charles Kaminski, sergeant, Co. M, Third cavalry, seriously. It was noticed that at the opening of the fight the shooting of the Indians was very wild, but a marked improvement in their aim was manifested toward the close. Bows and arrows were used in exceptional cases, but no wounds inflicted by them.

In charging into one of the tepees a man received a bullet through his cap. It just grazed his head, and as himself and a comrade or two rushed in to wreak their vengeance on the redskin who had fired, what was their astonishment at seeing three or four squaws, armed with revolvers, in the act of slipping through the opposite side of the wigwam, by way of a hole they had just carved with butcher knives.

These Indians may be cowardly, but they have a queer way of showing it. While in the extreme front we noticed a small band of ponies on our right that had been overlooked by the men detailed to gather them in. The main body of Indians was then on our left, and we were amazed to see a gaudily-dressed warrior, well mounted, emerge from behind a clump of bushes, tauntingly brandish his weapons, and start with break-neck speed toward the ponies, with the evident intention of making off with them. To accomplish this he was compelled to ride within two hundred yards of fifteen or twenty of us, and just before reaching the goal, faithful horse and reckless rider fell riddled with bullets.

Steward Bryan, of the Fort Fetterman hospital, who was with us on the charge, just after dismounting discovered a young warrior but a few yards distant with revolvers leveled over the top of a stump and in the act of shooting at him. The steward dodged behind his horse's head and the poor animal received the bullet in his brain. That Indian, it is generally believed, belonged to Lieutenant Bourke—although he denies the soft impeachment—as he was seen to look over the sights of his revolver in that direction about the time the audacious brave disappeared.

The village contained about 700 people, of whom the greater number were Sioux, who steal ponies from the frontier, go to the northern agencies and draw supplies, and also trade ponies there for arms and ammunition. There were also a few lodges of renegade Arapahoes.

Private Gouget, a Frenchman, of Captain Egan's company, while charging over rough ground on foot, fell, unnoticed, into a deep narrow pit. He was just tall enough to level his gun over the edge, and although the position was swept by the enemy's fire from three directions and there was no one to keep him company, he thought that a good place from which to fire some sixty rounds.

Private Murphy, company M, Third cavalry, had his gun stock shattered in his hands, and a pair of pantaloons ruined by the same ball. He now prefers carrying that broken gun and wearing those punctured pantaloons to getting a new outfit.

We failed to see the white girl who is known to be with this tribe. She was captured when only two or three years old, from Mormon emigrants, it is believed, and is now about twenty years of age. Frank Gruard, who, while a prisoner here saw her daily, says she is quite handsome, has a very pleasant disposition, and is esteemed and guarded as the richest treasure by her dusky companions. He never knew them to insult or maltreat her, and she is not obliged to perform any of the common labor of the squaws, most of her time being spent in doing fancy beadwork, embroidery, etc. Yet, not knowing a word of English, and having no knowledge of a more convenient sphere, she often, by her listless and unsatisfied manner, betrays a desire to leave the tribe, or at least to make some changes for the better.

Among the domestic animals about the village we noticed several broods of chickens and a number of fine dogs. The conduct of several of the latter seemed particularly strange. Lying by the sides of their masters' tepees when we arrived, they would not change their position one iota. As the domicle was torn down and it with its effects set on fire, the great faithful fellow would still remain motionless as a statue, heedless of coaxing, gazing wistfully and without a growl at the bands of destroyers.

General Crook, in ignorance of what has transpired, has failed to meet us here as yet, and while waiting we have time to take a hasty glance at the work of the last twenty-four hours. In spite of the fact that we have, in the midst of winter, thus found and routed from his own stronghold the second savage chieftain in importance, perhaps, in the whole western country, and have utterly wiped out his village and supplies, a number of very unpleasant conclusions here force themselves upon us. And it is only due the people who support the army and pride themselves in its efficiency, as well as to the brave and true soldier, who otherwise would suffer with the coward and the pretender, that these conclusions take the shape of words. Disguise it as we may, the fact still remains that owing to the failure yesterday of Captain A. Moore to take the position assigned him, a large proportion of the Indians were permitted to escape, thus rendering the victory incomplete in its most important detail; and, further, that through this same tardiness the situation of his brother officer, Captain Egan—who had charged into the heart of the enemy, in obedience to orders, with but a handful of men—was greatly imperiled. Then, in view of the fact that the troops were on half rations of meat, and that General Crook had instructed the officer in command to save all that could be carried off, the destruction of the large quantities of buffalo and venison not only deprived the troops of that which rightfully belonged to them, but also withheld from them that of which they now stand in great need. Also the leaving of the bodies of the dead, and one wounded man upon the field to fall into the hands of the red monsters, who, no doubt, immediately swept over it after our departure, seems utterly inexcusable, as there was no obstacle in the way of their prompt removal that could not have been surmounted by a battalion of troops. This grave oversight sounds all the worse from the fact that during the latter part of the engagement one battalion or squadron was permitted to unsaddle its animals, make coffee and partake of lunch in the very sight of the battlefield. Another point and I am done. After having captured some 700 ponies—by all odds the most important fruits of the victory—General Reynolds, in neglecting to either place a guard over them or to order their recapture when informed that the Indians were driving them away, certainly allowed the savages to equip themselves with the most important auxiliary to their future predatory incursions upon our frontier.

Chapter 2

The Skirmish at Tongue River Heights, June 9, 1876

Reuben Briggs Davenport

Following his reversal at Powder River, Crook fell back to Fort Fetterman to regroup his command and await improved weather conditions. He struck north again on May 29 as one component of a coordinated three-pronged movement into southeastern Montana Territory. The plan of converging columns was conceived by General Sheridan and envisioned trapping the Sioux and Northern Cheyennes in their summer haunts along the Powder, Tongue, Rosebud, and Big Horn rivers and their tributaries. Crook was to act in concert with a force headed by Brigadier General Alfred H. Terry from Fort Abraham Lincoln, Dakota Territory, and another commanded by Colonel John Gibbon from posts in western Montana.

Crook's column found the Indians first and skirmished with them near his bivouac on June 9. The episode proved but a portent for the major engagement on Rosebud Creek that followed eight days later. Both encounters were chronicled by Reuben Briggs Davenport, correspondent for the New York Herald. *In 1876, the native New Yorker was twenty-four years old but had garnered western experience the previous summer while serving on the Newton-Jenney expedition to the Black Hills. As another paper commented, "Davenport represents* The Herald; *and when we say represents we mean all that the word implies. His saddle, bridle, blankets, haversack, canteen, etc., are all marked conspicuously 'New York Herald.' He has not branded his horse 'Herald,' but he has got him so he looks like a* Herald *horse. In fact, everything about him goes to herald the fact that he represents* The Herald."

Because Davenport acquired a reputation for having a serious nose for news, he was occasionally victimized by officers and men who "perpetrated 'whoppers' on him." Nonetheless, his reports of the battle actions he witnessed have been shown to be precise recountings of impressive detail. His descriptions of the

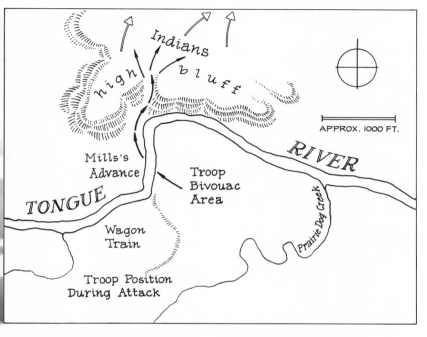

The Skirmish at Tongue River Heights, June 9, 1876.

*1876 expedition became progressively critical of Crook's perfor-
mance and caused the general considerable discomfort. In later years, Davenport was in the newspaper business variously in
Connecticut, Panama, and California, and during the Spanish-
American War he filed dispatches for the Associated Press from
Haiti, Jamaica, and Cuba. He spent several years in Europe during and after World War I and eventually settled in Montpellier,
France, where he died in 1932 at age eighty. Davenport's account of Crook's fight with the Indians along Tongue River
appeared in the* New York Herald *on June 16, 1876.*

THIS BODY OF TROOPS HAD MARCHED 100 consecutive
miles on June 7, when Tongue River was reached, and then
they rested three days. Until then no unequivocal signs of

Indians had been seen, although puffs of smoke rose above the eastern horizon. Part of these signals were made by a party of miners from Montana, who were examining gulches in search of gold near Pumpkin Bull [Butte] and removing toward the Black Hills. Their recent camping grounds were found, where they had erected redoubts for defence against Indians, with whom they had probably had skirmishes.

On the night of our arrival at Tongue River Camp we were aroused at twelve o'clock by a loud declamation delivered by a sombre figure walking on the top of the bluffs on the north bank, opposite General Crook's headquarters. Other figures from time to time appeared and harangued successively during an hour. As nearly as could be comprehended, they announced the destruction of the invading force if not withdrawn, and warned us of a formidable attack before two suns should roll around. They asked us, as if in irony, if the Crows had joined the troops; and now some fear is felt lest harm may have come to the guides sent to Montana Agency to gain their alliance, who have not yet returned. After this visitation the camp was strongly picketed, but a day and night succeeded the savage menaces with only a slight false alarm. The day before yesterday, at about four o'clock in the afternoon, the infantry picket saw about fifty Indians on the bluff opposite the camp, stealing to positions behind the rocks. The infantry fired upon them and the camp was alarmed. Though surprised they immediately returned the fire with yells. A hundred flashes were instantly seen along the crest of the ridge, and several mounted warriors rode out in full view, circling rapidly; and there was instantly heard another sharp fusillade. A volley from the camp was poured into the bluff. The pickets on every side were strengthened and the herd secured, in anticipation of any attempt that might be made to capture it. Half a mile up the river a band of Sioux tried

Attack of the Indians on Crook's camp along the upper Tongue River, June 9, 1876. From *Frank Leslie's Popular Monthly*, September 1890.

to cross, but were driven back by the prompt attention of the pickets. Indians were seen at the same time on the south side of the camp, but they remained distant. A battalion, under the command of Captain [Anson] Mills, Third cavalry, advanced rapidly across the river, dismounted in a grove under the bluff and charged up the deep ravine. The first man to reach the top saw two hundred Indians, moving incessantly on ponies, but slowly receding. The troops, stretching out in a skirmish line, drove them back in the face of a brisk fire, which they answered wherever redskins were visible above sagebrush, behind which they sought to screen themselves. They seemed bold and confident, and when a feint of retiring was executed by the troops they quickly changed their retreat to an advance. It is supposed they had a large reserve massed in the ravines and expected to entice the small party into a pursuit, so as to surround and annihilate them.

When they saw the full strength of the cavalry they finally retreated. One of the party of Indians, on attempting to cross the river, was shot, and was lifted from his seat by his companions. Those on the bluff led off the riderless pony.

It was supposed that two Indians were wounded or killed, at least. No soldier engaged in the fight was injured, but two in the camp suffered contusions from spent balls. Three horses and one mule were killed.

Intelligence has been received by our commander of the probable coming of 120 Shoshones as auxiliaries, under Washakie, the chief. Their arrival is expected every day, and active aggressive operations only await the coming of these Indian allies.

General Crook is informed that 3,000 more warriors have deserted the Red Cloud Agency, proceeding north on the warpath. It will probably be his policy to prevent them finding refuge there again if whipped, until they sue for peace and surrender their arms. The presence of the Fifth cavalry there is to enforce this plan.

In consequence of the unsafe position of the camp on Tongue River the expedition marched to-day [June 11] sixteen miles to this point [on Goose Creek], which will be made the base of supplies.

Chapter 3

The Battle of Rosebud Creek, June 17, 1876

Reuben Briggs Davenport

On June 20, Davenport filed his description of Crook's battle with the Sioux and Cheyennes along the headwaters of Rosebud Creek. In this report he criticized both Crook's direction of affairs and the role of the Crow scouts. It appeared in the New York Herald *on July 6, 1876.*

THREE DAYS AGO THE FIRST FIGHT of the campaign against the Sioux in this military department took place. The fighting column marched from the camp, situated at the fork of Goose Creek, on June 16, accompanied by the 250 Indian auxiliaries who had arrived on the preceding day, and numbered about 1,300 men. The infantry were mounted upon mules borrowed from the pack trains. Twenty mounted packers were also allowed to go, and carried carbines. The cavalry battalions contained 832 able soldiers. The friendly Indians were loaned firearms belonging to the government and their belts filled with cartridges. Old Crow was the principal leader of the Crows, and Medicine Crow and Good Heart his lieutenants. Louissant [Luishaw], called by his tribe "Weesaw," was the chief of the Snakes, or Soshonees [Shoshones], who are divided into two companies, regularly disciplined in imitation of the white soldiers. Louissant is captain of one and [Tom] Cosgrove, a white man, commands the other. They march sometimes in column, and nearly every Soshonee, in going to war, carries a long white wand ornamented with pennants or streamers of fur, hair and red cloth. They wear parti-colored blankets, and ride usually either white or spotted ponies, whose tails and manes they daub with red or orange paint. Nothing could be more bright and picturesque than the whole body of friendly Indians as they galloped by the long column of the expedition early in the first morning of the march, as it wound around the bases of the low foot hills called the Chetish or Wolf Mountains, which were traversed in moving toward the head waters of Rosebud Creek. Several of the Snakes still carry their ancient spears and round shields of buffalo horn and elk hide, besides their modern firearms. Imagination did not require more than the presence of the brown arid hills and the distant snow-capped mountains to convert them into a cavalcade of Bedouins. After crossing the sterile hills and leaving behind them stunted thorns and cedars the column stretched like a great serpent over a green divide, whose surface is undulating as billows of mid-ocean, and which separates the watersheds of the Tongue River and the Rosebud Creek. The country is beautiful. The march was silent as possible, and the column was dispersed so as to avoid causing dust, which might give warning to the enemy. It was hoped to approach within thirty miles of the Sioux village and then to advance on it during the night.

After a weary march of thirty-five miles the column bivouacked at the head of the valley of the Rosebud on June 16. The soldiers placed their blankets so that in sleeping their lines formed a hollow square, inside of which the animals were picketed.

On the morning of June 17 the command moved at five o'clock. The Crow scouts went in front and on the flanks, but they had omitted to send forward their spies during the night, although on the previous day they had found indubitable signs that the Sioux were then engaged in hunting the buffalo southward. About half-past seven an advance of ten miles had been made, when, suddenly, the Old Crow appeared on a hill near the stream, and gave a signal. Soon other scouts dashed into the valley. Meanwhile the Crows were catching their war ponies, stripping off their superfluous garments, and some of them had formed in line and were singing their war song. A halt had been made at the first signal of the scouts, and the order was given to unsaddle the animals, it being supposed that they had merely seen some of the Sioux, near their village upon the hills, engaged in herding their ponies. The two battalions of the Third cavalry were resting on the south side of the creek and the one of the Second on the north side. Suddenly yells were heard beyond the low hill on the north, and shots were fired, which every moment were becoming more frequent. The Crows were wild with excitement, and shouted to the interpreters that their scouts were being killed and that they must go to join them. After circling on their ponies in the valley for ten minutes they dashed over the hill and disappeared. The firing became more and more rapid. The cavalry were making ready to mount, when scouts came galloping back again, hallooing that the Sioux were charging.

General Crook rode to the first crest and saw that they were coming forward to attack the whole command in the valley. Orders were given Colonel [Lieutenant Colonel William B.] Royall to lead the battalions of the Third cavalry across the stream, deploy his troops as skirmishers and occupy the hills in the possession of the enemy. Captain [Guy V.] Henry's battalion of the Third cavalry, consisting of Companies D, B, L and F, advanced northward up a series of ridges occupied by the Indians, who retired before the steady charge from point to point. At last was reached the top of a ridge lying adjacent to the highest crest, but separated from it by a deep ravine. The Sioux were in front and were promptly attacked. They occupied also a palisade on the left, about 800 yards distant. Captain [William H.] Andrews' company had become detached from its battalion and had advanced on the extreme left, and it was employed in checking an early flanking movement of the Indians. Colonel Royall, in advancing, had crossed and left behind him the deep hollow west of the main ridge on which the Sioux first appeared and back over which they had been driven by a line of infantry to a higher crest, stopping its northern extremity.

The troops were going forward with an ardor and enthusiasm which found vent in cheers, and their officers were surprised to observe that they were receiving no support from the centre, which was yielding ground and permitting the enemy to turn their fire against the right flank. After checking the advance behind a friendly crest behind which his soldiers lay while pouring into the Sioux a hot answering fire, Colonel Royall was expectant of seeing the advance on his right resumed, as the latter were then apparently beginning to feel a panic. Seeing the long gallant skirmish line pause, however, they dashed forward on the right and left, and in an instant nearly every point of vantage within, in front and in the rear, and on the flank of the line, was covered with savages wildly circling their ponies and charging hither and thither, while they fired from their seats with wonderful rapidity and accuracy.

At this moment the loss to the troops commenced. They opened a severe fire upon the Indians, which was seen to have instant effect, but a cry arose that they were the Crows, and immediately it was checked. Thus was lost an excellent opportunity for punishing them severely. They screened themselves behind elevations and continued a harassing fire. Still the troops on the right did not advance, and the suspense grew terrible as the position was every moment more perilous as the Sioux appeared at intervals on the left flank, charging on their ponies and each time further toward the rear. In the meantime they swept down into the valley where the command had halted in the morning at the first alarm, directly behind the left wing, and, killing a Snake, captured a small herd of ponies which

Brigadier General George Crook, who commanded the Big Horn and Yellowstone expedition in 1876. Courtesy of Paul L. Hedren.

Romantic portrayal of the cavalry charging at Rosebud Creek, June 17, 1876. From Richard Irving Dodge, *Our Wild Indians: Thirty-three Years' Personal Experience Among the Red Men of the Great West* (Hartford: A. D. Worthington and Company, 1881).

he was guarding. Lieutenant [James E. H.] Foster, with a squad of men from Captain Andrews' company, was sent to cut off the Sioux and recapture the ponies. He dashed after them two miles and only halted when he found the enemy springing up so thickly around him that he feared it would be impossible to fight his way back. In rejoining the left wing he rode through a series of ravines, and in emerging from them at full gallop was unfortunately mistaken for a party of the enemy and three volleys were fired at him by the troops. No damage was done to his men.

As Colonel Royall was determining to make a rapid charge on the heights held by the Sioux, and by desperately dislodging them, extricating himself from his exposed position, Captain [Azor H.] Nickerson, aide-de-camp, having made a wide circuit around the hollow lying between the General's headquarters and Colonel Royall's line, dashed down a steep side hill under a concentrated fire, the bullets making the dust fly under his horse's hoofs, and delivered the unexpected order to fall back. The line on the main ridge, backed by a mass of cavalry and infantry, still remained stationary. To retreat into the hollow on the right, which would be necessary in order to form a junction with the centre, was to risk the certain loss of nearly the whole battalion. Colonel Royall, however, obeyed his order to extend his line in that direction by sending Captain [Charles] Meinhold's company of the Third cavalry around by such a route as saved it from much exposure and then slowly receded from crest to crest, keeping a strong line of skirmishers continually deployed to amuse the enemy. As the retreat progressed they obtained better range upon the troops at every moment, but the skirmishers did their utmost in firing coolly and with steady aim. It cannot be doubted that their bullets took effect among the savages crowded on the high point of the main ridge. Many were seen to fall and subsequently several dead ponies strewed the ground. The horses belonging to the dismounted cavalrymen were led first into the small ravines in the bottom of the valley.

At this juncture the soldiers felt great discouragement, but preserved their coolness, although death had just begun his work among them, a murderous enfilading fire causing them to drop every moment. Captain [Peter D.] Vroom, Lieutenant [Charles] Morton and Lieutenant [Henry R.] Lemley [Lemly], of the Third cavalry, took places in the skirmish line when the enemy were within range, and used their carbines with effect. Unwilling to let slip an opportunity for helping the extrication of the left line, with which my own fate was identified by the chance of battle, I dismounted at several points during our retreat and fired with the skirmishers. At last, when the receding line reached the last ridge next the fatal hollow, it became evident that the sacrifice of a few lives was inevitable for the salvation of many more. Colonel Royall sent his adjutant, Lieutenant Lemley, through the storm of bullets to ask a support of infantry to protect his retreat. About the same moment Captain Guy V. Henry, who had remained at the head of his battalion under the hottest fire, was horribly wounded in the face. He was lifted from his horse and led to the rear by two of his soldiers. The tide of retreat now grew more excited and turbulent, and I was pressed back, with the soldier attending me, over the rearward crest upon the slope, which was raked by an oblique fire from the north.

The infantry which was expected to relieve this line was not in position soon enough to check the wild advance of the Sioux, who, observing the retiring body becoming crowded together on the edge of the gap which it must cross under fire, rushed both down and up the valley on the right while they poured their fire from the high bluff across the low elevation, rendering it utterly untenable, while they were charging at the same time to prevent its abandonment. A swarm of Sioux were within 1,000 yards of me in front and I heard their shots in the rear as they murdered the poor soldiers of the rear guard of the retreat. I was obliged either to take the chance of death then or wait to cross with the battalion, which would attract a still more fatal fire, because it would form a large mark for the aim of the enemy. The hill where the General's headquarters were and a large body of troops which had not yet been engaged was more than half a mile distant. I chose the converging ravines and rode through them a greater part of the way, but as I galloped up the slope opposite the one I had left I heard the yells of the savages close behind, and the reports of their rifles, as I emerged from the safer ground, sounded remarkably near and loud.

Looking behind I saw a dozen Sioux surrounding a group of soldiers who had straggled behind the retreat. Six were killed at one spot. A recruit surrendered his carbine to a painted warrior, who flung it to the ground, and cleft his head with a stroke of the tomahawk. William W. Allen, a brave, old soldier, who had been twenty years in the army, fought with magnificent courage, and was killed. The Sioux rode so close to their victims that they shot them in the face with revolvers and the powder blackened the flesh. Captains [Thomas B.] Burrow's [Burrowes's] and [Andrew S.] Burt's companies of infantry by this time were firing well directed volleys from a position half way down the west side of the high bluff, and just after my escape the Snake Indians, gallantly led by their chiefs, Louissant and Cosgrove, dashed with thrilling shouts into the hollow, among the Sioux who were on the rear of the cavalry, and drove them back. Captain Henry, weak from the bleeding of his wound, had been unable to keep up with the retreat and had sunk on the ground. Louissant put himself astride the body and for five minutes kept the Sioux off, when some soldiers of his company rushed back and rescued him. About the same time a corporal of F company, of the Third cavalry, made a last charge, with three men, and captured from the enemy the bodies of their comrades, thus saving them from the scalping knife. The Snakes took two scalps from the Sioux whom they killed in the hollow, and swung them, fresh and bleeding, with gleeful triumph above their heads as they returned. The infantry under Captains Burrows and Burt executed their part admirably.

It remains to be said of the portion of the engagement which I have thus far described that it was the most important and dangerous, and that in it Captain Henry's battalion of the Third cavalry and Captain Andrews' company of the Second cavalry, with all their officers, displayed a most honorable degree of fortitude and bravery. They had a more arduous duty and suffered more severely than any other portion of the command. Colonel Royall was circumscribed by orders in every one of his movements, and the disaster attending the retreat would have been much greater had it not been so skillfully directed by him. On the left of his line was a lofty crescent-shaped palisade, toward which, early in the morning, he deployed skirmishers. Had the order to fall back been a little later this would have been occupied. It would then have been impossible for the Sioux to have circled around to the rear, and a fire could have been turned upon the last high point held by them, which would have compelled them to hide behind it, while the cavalry could have charged up the hollow and reached them before they could realize their predicament. Then the soldiers could have dismounted and fired such volleys as would have ended the fight and made a chase.

It is now time to glance at the other portions of the field, where there were three times as many troops as were on the left, and yet where there was hardly any fighting, except that done by successive lines of skirmishers, which held the southern end of the great ridge.

In the morning, after the Crows and Snakes had rushed forward to meet the Sioux, Captain [Avery B.] Kane's [Cain's] company of infantry was first ordered for-

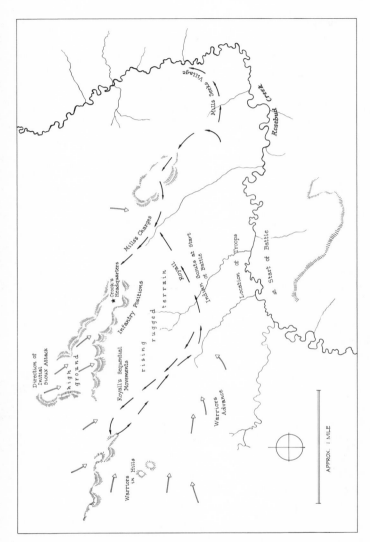

The Battle of Rosebud Creek, June 17, 1876.

ward to the top of the nearest hill. From that point it commenced firing. The Sioux were seen in great numbers
beyond, covering every summit, and were engaged with
the friendly Indians in a warm fusillade. The infantry advanced toward the high ridge, resting upon each successive elevation, which they mounted to discharge volleys
into the groups of the enemy occupying still higher points.
Captain [Henry B.] Noyes, in command of the battalion of
the Second cavalry, composed of companies A, B, D, E and
I, saw the importance of carrying a portion of the main
ridge immediately before they could advance further south
and attack the column in the valley, where a portion of the
cavalry was not yet mounted. He, therefore, advanced before receiving any orders, passed the right flank of the
infantry and took a knoll beyond them.

The friendly Indians had been carried by the impetu-
osity of their first charge far beyond the front of the infantry, and a party of the Snakes seemed to be fighting
independently on a cone-shaped mound, just visible two
miles away. As the sequel showed, they killed and scalped
a small party of Sioux there, and held their ground until the
troops advanced beyond them. The Crows and the rest of
the Snakes were between the troops and the Sioux, and it
was feared that the bullets intended for the latter would
strike our allies. After great shouting by the interpreters of
General Crook's wishes they retired running, as if in flight.
The Sioux, as well as the cavalry on the left, mistook the
movements, and the former became extremely bold and
advanced in swarms. It was then that Colonel Royall's line
found itself too far ahead in the very midst of the enemy.
Captain Mills' battalion of the Third cavalry, composed of
companies A, E, I and M, which had been ordered to make
the first charge, now advanced through the battalion of the
Second cavalry, deployed in a skirmish line and charged
the point above where the smoke of the Indian rifles was
growing dense. It was carried with inspiriting shouts, and

the Sioux ran back to another, still higher, apex. The hostile lines were here face to face, although each availed itself of the protection of the stony summits. Volley after volley was exchanged between them, and the Sioux lost several of their warriors. General Crook saw thirteen of them fall.

Early in the engagement a squadron of the Third cavalry, comprising companies C and G, under command of Captain [Frederick] Van Vliet, had occupied a steep bluff on the south side of the stream to protect the troops in the bottom while they were saddling their horses. It was withdrawn as soon as the whole command was engaged in the forward movement, and was now posted on the high ridge, dismounted and ready for action in the rear of Captain Mills' line. The Indians meanwhile were flocking to a butte northeast of this position, and had opened fire upon it.

Captain Mills received an order to wheel his battalion to the right, advance a furlong, then wheel to the left and charge the steep incline. It was executed with rapidity, and the summit carried, but not until the enemy before dispersing had delivered three heavy volleys at the advancing line. The battalion, after halting on the bluff, was ordered by General Crook to advance directly through the canyon of the stream northward, toward the supposed locality of the Sioux village. By transposition of the forces, it now formed the right of the command, and the Second cavalry battalion was ordered to follow it as a support. The General directed that the battle in progress should be ignored by this wing of the command and that it should capture and destroy the village. Frank Gruard was ordered to ride in the front and select the route of march. It was expected that the tepees of the bands of Sitting Bull and Crazy Horse would be found only ten miles distant. Hardly had the first battalion moved away when Captain Noyes was sent a counter order, based upon a new report brought to General Crook by a Crow, that the village was in an exactly opposite direction. Captain Nickerson, aide and acting as-

·sistant adjutant general, was dispatched at full gallop to check Captain Mills' advance, and overtook him only after a chase of five miles, during which he was accompanied by a solitary orderly. The two battalions recalled were ordered to positions to protect the rear and command the valley where the morning halt had been made.

The Indians, after the withdrawal of Captain Mills' battalion from the long ridge, had regained the crest which he evacuated, and engaged Van Vliet's squadron at the same time that they poured a terrible fire into Colonel Royall's line on the left, compelling him, after holding his position at a disadvantage so long and with such brave retaliation, to order at last a rapid retreat across a deep defile, with the enemy charging both flanks and the rear. This was the last effort of the Sioux. The infantry and Snakes drove them steadily back from the moment that the left wing emerged from its race of the gantlet.

After the firing had ceased the whole force was concentrated, and it advanced in pursuit of the Indians. It was observed, however, that the Crows remained behind on the summit of a hill, where they were holding a pow-wow. They had captured a pony from the Sioux, which they had left at home in their village and they feared lest it had been attacked during their absence. They also desired to take back two of their braves who were wounded, and to condole with the squaw of a young Snake who belonged to their band and who was killed. General Crook, on learning of their disaffection, determined to return to the point where the battle began and to rest there until evening, so that the Crows might fully determine what they would do. They told him, at length, that they could not stay, but must have their war dance at home over the scalps which they had won. Believing that the Sioux village had been removed during the fight, and dreading to march forward through so rough a country after the desertion of his scouts, General Crook determined in the morning to move back toward Goose Creek. The object of the scout, which was so unsuccessful and yet not without an encouraging result, was to discover and destroy the village of the Sioux, which the guides, while half-breed and Indian, agreed in declaring to be on the Yellowstone River, between the mouths of the Rosebud and the Tongue. It proved to be nearer the base of the expedition than was believed, and General Crook's ignorance of its proximity, due to the negligence and inactivity of the Crow allies, who were intrusted with the work of scouting, is the cause of the failure of the movement. The Sioux were certainly repulsed in their bold and confident onset, and lost many of their bravest warriors, but, when they fled, could not be pursued without great danger in the rough country through which their way lay.

Had his scouts proved faithful, so that he could have been prepared to occupy the commanding positions with infantry in advance of the main column, he would have had warning of the concentration of the enemy to impede his course, and could have driven him back into his village and ended the campaign by destroying it. It will be seen that the blame of the miscarriage of the scout belongs to the Crows, whose instincts, vigilance and knowledge of their own country was relied upon to render every move of the force intelligent. On the contrary, their undisciplined frenzy and failure to discover the lodgment of the enemy in time to frustrate their meditated attack precipitated a battle which began with a stupendous advantage on his side and in a spot of his own choice naturally suitable to the success of their method of warfare. The Sioux's strength was masked, except when, emboldened by the disastrous withdrawal of the left wing of the cavalry, they made a dash from both ends of a deep hollow which lay in its way and exposed it to a murderous fire, and suddenly swarmed on the front, left and rear. Then it was that the timely fire of the infantry upon their main body, the charge of the Snakes into the hollow and rapid pursuit of them for three miles, dismayed them utterly and they fell back and disappeared. Had it not been for their occupation, unperceived by the General, of positions from which they could pour an enfilading fire upon both flanks of the body of cavalry on the left, they would not have stood in the face of the troops a moment after their first charge. The injury inflicted upon them must have been much greater than that which we suffered. Their loss of lives is estimated at about one hundred. There is no doubt that all the northern Sioux warriors were engaged in the battle, and it is believed that they have been severely crippled.

Chapter 4

The Battle of the Little Big Horn, June 25–26, 1876

William Jackson

While Crook's force engaged the Sioux and Cheyennes at Rose-
bud Creek, events proceeded to the north that would culminate
in the Battle of the Little Big Horn, one of the few utterly crush-
ing defeats experienced by U.S. troops at the hands of Indian
warriors. Brigadier General Alfred H. Terry's column from Fort
Abraham Lincoln included the Seventh Cavalry commanded by
Lieutenant Colonel George A. Custer. Scouting through the
Powder River country in mid-June, soldiers under Custer's sub-
ordinate, Major Marcus A. Reno, came upon a large Indian trail
leading west. Reno reported his discovery to Terry and Custer,
who were unaware of Crook's setback on June 17. On June 22,
Terry directed Custer to march up Rosebud Creek, strike the
trail, and exercise discretion in advancing toward a major village
suspected to be located in Little Big Horn Valley. Terry, with
Colonel John Gibbon's column, would march west along the Yel-
lowstone before ascending the Big Horn and Little Big Horn
rivers to reach the anticipated proximity of Custer's command.

One of the Indian scouts with Custer was William, or Billy,
Jackson, a mixed-blood of Pikuni Blackfoot heritage. In June
1876 he was only nineteen years old. Jackson had been born at
Fort Benton, Montana, and had seen frequent service as a scout,
most recently enlisting in December 1875. He had participated
in the Yellowstone expedition of 1873 and the Black Hills expe-
dition of the following year. At the Battle of the Little Big Horn,
Jackson accompanied his older brother, Robert, with Reno's bat-
talion. Billy Jackson died in 1901 on the Blackfoot Reservation,
Montana. His highly personalized account of the Little Big Horn
fight was given to his friend, James Willard Schultz, who
recorded it in William Jackson, Indian Scout, *published in 1926.*
The following excerpt from that book begins with Custer's depar-
ture from the mouth of Rosebud Creek.

William Jackson, mixed-blood scout for Custer and other commanders during the Great Sioux War. Courtesy of Historical Collections/University Archives, University of Colorado at Boulder Libraries.

GENERAL [LIEUTENANT COLONEL] CUSTER, with his Seventh Cavalry, a pack train carrying fifteen days' rations and extra cartridges, his own scouts, and six Crow scouts under John Bruyer [Mitch Bouyer], from Gibbon's command, left the mouth of the Rosebud about noon, June 22d. My brother and I rode with an old friend of ours, Frank [Fred] Girard [Gerard], a man who had once been captured by Crazy Horse's band of Sioux, and had lived with them so long that he had acquired no little of their ways, and their religion.

On the third day, we struck the trail of the hostiles, the one that Reno had found several days before. And what a trail it was; a trail all of three hundred yards wide, and deeply worn by travois, and lodge-pole ends. We went into camp close to the trail, and, cooking our supper, we scouts counciled together about the outlook. All agreed that at least fifteen hundred lodges of the enemy had made that broad trail. Said [the Arikara scout] Bloody Knife: "My friends, this big trail proves what we heard, that the Ogalalla, Minneconjou, Sans Arc, and Teton Sioux have left their agencies to join Sitting Bull and Crazy Horse; but I am sure that even this trail does not account for all that have left their agencies. There surely are other trails of them; and trails, too, of Cheyennes and Arapahoes."

"Many Yanktonnais and Assiniboin have answered Sitting Bull's call for help, and joined him," said Frank Girard.

"Yes. They too," Bloody Knife continued. "It is as I have told Long Hair: this gathering of the enemy tribes is too many for us. But he will not believe me. He is bound to lead us against them. They are not far away; just over this ridge, they are all encamped and waiting for us. Crazy Horse and Sitting Bull are not men-without-sense; they have their scouts out, and some of them surely have their eyes upon us. Well, to-morrow we are going to have a big fight, a losing fight. Myself, I know what is to happen to me; my sacred helper has given me warning that I am not to see the set of to-morrow's sun."

Sad words, those. They chilled us. I saw [scout] Charlie Reynolds nod agreement to them, and was chilled again when he said in a low voice: "I feel as he does: tomorrow will be the end for me, too. Any one who wants my little outfit of stuff"—pointing to his war sack—"can have it right now." He opened it, began passing out tobacco; a sewing-kit; several shirts and so on. Many refused the presents; those who accepted them did so with evident reluctance.

We had little appetite for our coffee and hardtack, and the meat that we were broiling. While we were eating, word was passed from mess to mess to put out the fires. That was quickly done, and soon afterward, Lieutenant [Charles A.] Varnum, who was in charge of the scouts, came over and said that it was General Custer's plan to attempt a surprise attack upon the camp of the enemy. The command was to rest until about midnight, and then again take the trail; some of us scouts, meantime, were to push on ahead and try to locate the camp.

Said Bloody Knife: "We cannot surprise the enemy! They are not crazy; without doubt their scouts have watched every move that we have made."

"Well, Bloody Knife, that is probably true, but we must try to surprise them, must we not?"

"Yes, o' course. We try!" he replied.

"Very well. We will go out in three parties: Bryer, you take two of your Crows and go forward on the right of the trail. Bloody Knife, you take the left of the trail, with two of your Rees. You Jackson boys, and you, Reynolds, come with me on the trail," ordered Varnum.

We saddled our horses, mounted, and struck out all together. We kept together for all of a mile, and then Bruyer and the Crows and Bloody Knife and the Rees branched off and left us to follow the trail. We moved on cautiously, often stopping to listen for the barking of camp dogs in answer to the howling of the wolves, and to look for the red gleam of sparks from some sick one's lodge-fire. So we went on and on through the night, getting no sight or sound of the enemy. At dawn, the command overtook us, and Lieutenant Varnum reported to General Custer. There we rested and had some breakfast.

While we were eating, several of the packers rode swiftly up through the command to General Custer, and we soon learned that they had lost a box of hardtack off one of the mules, and, on going back, had found some Indians around it, stuffing the contents into their clothing. None could now doubt that the enemy had all along kept watch of our advance. With a grim laugh, Charlie Reynolds said to me: "I knew well enough that they had scouts ahead of us, but I didn't think that others would be trailing along to pick up stuff dropped by our careless packers."

Convinced at last that we could not possibly surprise the enemy, General Custer ordered a quick advance, with the scouts and himself in the lead. We had not gone far when Bloody Knife and his two Rees joined us, and reported that on the other side of the ridge they had found the day-old trail of many more of the enemy going toward the valley of the Little Bighorn.

On we went over the divide. We soon met John Bruyer and his two Crows. They were excited, and Bruyer said to Custer: "General, we have discovered the camp, down there on the Little Horn. It is a big one! Too big for you to tackle! Why, there are thousands and thousands of Sioux and Cheyennes down there."

For a moment the general stared at him, angrily, I thought, and then sternly replied: "I shall attack them! If you are afraid, Bruyer—"

"I guess I can go wherever you do," Bruyer quickly answered; and at that, the general turned back to the command, we following him. He had the bugler sound the

Lieutenant Colonel George A. Custer, Seventh U.S. Cavalry. Courtesy of Little Bighorn Battlefield National Monument.

officers' call, and the command rested while they got together, and Custer gave his orders for the attack upon the
camp.

None of the scouts had been far in the lead, and they
all came in. Rees and Crows and whites and Robert and I,
we were a gathering of solemn faces. Speaking in English,
and the sign language, too, so that all would understand,
Bruyer described the enemy camp. It was, he said, all of
three miles long, and made up of hundreds and hundreds
of lodges. Above it and below and west of it were thousands
and thousands of horses that were being close-herded.
With his few riders, Long Hair had decided to attack the
camp, and we were going to have a terrible fight; we should
all take courage, fight hard, make our every shot a killer.
He finished, and none spoke. But after a minute or two,
Bloody Knife looked up and signed to Sun: "I shall not see
you go down behind the mountains to-night." And at that I
almost choked. I felt that he knew that his end was near,
that there was no escaping it. I turned and looked the other
way. I thought that my own end was near. I felt very sad.

The officers' council did not last long, and, when it
ended, Lieutenant Varnum came hurrying to us scouts and
said that the command was going to split up to make the
attack on the camp, and that we were to go with Major
Reno's column, down the trail of the hostiles that we had
been following from the Rosebud. We were soon in the
saddle and headed down a narrow valley toward the river.

Bruyer told us that the big camp of the enemy was
well below the foot of the narrow valley and on the other
side of the Little Bighorn. We crossed the river, turned
straight down the valley, went down it for more than a
mile, and saw some of the enemy retreating before our
advance. A grove of timber in a bend below prevented our
seeing their camp. As we neared the timber, we heard a
single shot fired beyond it, and then the Indians began firing at us. We then went on, and, passing the timber, saw a

great camp, and a horde of riders coming up from it to attack us. We all turned into the timber then, and got our horses into an old timber and brush dry channel of the river.

Within two minutes from the time that we left our horses, and climbed up the bank from them, we had a line of defense in the brush and out across toward the west bluff of the valley. Then came the rush of the enemy, all of five hundred well-mounted riders in all their war finery, eager to get at us. Their shots, their war-cries, the thunder of their horses feet were deafening.

It was the intention of the enemy to charge straight through the center of our line, but, by the time they had come within fifty yards, we had shot so many of them that they swung out and went streaming past the outer end of our line, lying low upon their horses and firing rapidly. The dust that their swift charge raised—the ground was very dry—almost choked us: it drifted upon us like a thick fog, and obscured the sun.

As the enemy were coming straight at our line, Robert, at my side in the brush, exclaimed, "Look! That one on the big white horse! He's Black Elk!"

So he was Black Elk, our enemy of the Round Butte and Fort Buford. We both fired at him, our shots apparently missing, but, just as he with the others was swerving off to flank us, he suddenly pitched head first from his horse, and Robert shouted to me: "I got him!"

Several hundred of the enemy went thundering past that outer end of our line, and, swinging in, began attack upon our rear; others were starting to cut us off from the river, and more and more arrivals from the camp swarmed in front of us. I thought that we were about to meet our end right there, every one of us. Then an officer ordered us in to our horses. By the time we got to them, we were entirely surrounded. As we mounted, a man right beside me fell dead out of his saddle. I saw Bloody Knife, Reynolds, and

Girard all getting upon their horses. I saw Major Reno, hatless, a handkerchief tied around his head, getting up on his plunging horse. Waving his six-shooter, he shouted something that I couldn't hear, and led swiftly off, up out of the depression that we were in. We all swarmed after him, and headed back up the way that we had come, our intention being to recross the river and get up onto the bluffs, where we could make a stand. By this time hundreds more of the enemy had come up from the camp, and all together they swarmed in on us and a hand-to-hand fight with them began.

I saw numbers of our men dropping from their horses, saw horses falling, heard their awful neighs of fright and pain. Close ahead of me, Bloody Knife, and then Charlie Reynolds, went down, right there met the fate that they had foretold.

A big heavy-set Indian brushed up against me, tried to pull me out of the saddle, and I shot him. Then, right in front, a soldier's horse was shot from under him, and as I came up, he grasped my right stirrup and ran beside me. I had to check my horse so that he could keep up, and so began to lag behind. Numbers of Indians were passing on both sides of us, eager to get at the main body of the retreat. At last one of the passing Indians made a close shot at the soldier and killed him, and, as I gave my horse loose rein, Frank Girard came up on my left, and we rode on side by side. Ahead, there was now a solid body of Indians between us and the retreating, hard-pressed soldiers, and Girard shouted to me: "We can't go through them! Let's turn back!"

Indians were still coming on from the direction of their camp, and, as we wheeled off to the left, and then went quartering back toward the timber, several of them shot at us, but we finally got into thick, high brush, dismounted and tied our horses. Just then we saw some one coming toward us, and were about to fire at him when we discovered that he was Lieutenant [Charles C.] De Rudio. He told us that his horse had run away from him. As we stood there, listening to the heavy firing up on the river, we were joined by [Private] Thomas O'Neil, of Company G, also horseless.

Lieutenant De Rudio asked that Girard and I put our horses farther back in the brush, and then all four look for a hiding-place. We did that, and were soon lying in a small, round, sandy depression surrounded by brush, about twenty yards from the open flat, up which a few Indians were still hurrying from the camp below. We lay each of us facing a different direction.

The sound of the fighting up the river seemed to be farther and farther from us. We learned later that, after we were cut off from the retreat, the enemy, at least a thousand of them against Reno's one hundred, drove the troops down a steep bank into the river and began following them across it. On the other side was a very high, steep bank, and some of the troops managed to get up onto it and check the Indians until the remaining troops got up, when they all went to the top of the main bluffs and there made a stand, and were there joined by [Captain Frederick W.] Benteen and his three companies, and then by [Captain Thomas B.] MacDougall and the pack train. They then went north along the bluffs, to try to find General Custer's column and join it, but were driven back to the point from which they started.

Great numbers of the enemy now went down the flat in front of us, riding fast, and we heard heavy firing away down the valley and knew that they were fighting Custer there. The sun beat down upon us, and we began to suffer from heat and thirst. Women from the camp came up on horseback, on foot, and leading travois-horses, and began carrying off their dead and wounded, and stripping our dead of their clothing, and slashing their bodies. That was a tough sight. Said O'Neil: "That's the way they will cut us up if they get us."

Artistic portrayal of Custer's Last Stand at the Little Big Horn by
A. R. Waud. From Edward S. Ellis, *The Indian Wars of the
United States* (Chicago: J. D. Kenyon and Company, 1892).

"But does it matter what happens to our bodies after we die! The point is, we mustn't die!" Girard exclaimed.

As the day wore on, we suffered terribly from want of water. We seldom spoke to one another; just watched and suffered.

When night came, we decided to try to make our way to the remains of our column, several miles up the river, and on the bluffs on the opposite side. Girard and I were to ride our horses, the others walking close at our side. Then, if we were discovered, De Rudio and O'Neil were to drop down flat upon the ground, and we were to ride away, drawing the enemy after us.

We were no sooner out of the brush than we began to pass the bodies of the men and horses that had been killed along the line of Reno's retreat. The men had all been stripped of their clothing, and were so badly cut up that, try as I would, I could not force myself to see if my brother were one of the slain.

We went on to the river, coming to a halt at the edge of a bank dropping straight down to the water; on the other side, a high, black, and very steep bank faced us. Close under us the current was swift but noiseless, and we doubted that it was fordable. O'Neil jumped in to ascertain the depth, went in almost to his neck and would have been carried downstream had he not seized some overhanding brush and drawn himself to footing closer in. He filled his hat with water and passed it up to De Rudio, who handed it to me. I drank every drop it contained and wanted more. After the hat had been filled and passed up again and again, De Rudio got down into the stream to test its current and depth, and soon agreed with O'Neil that it was too swift and deep for us to ford. We went on up the shore, looking for a place to cross.

Back of us, down the valley, the enemy had built many fires in the open, and were singing, dancing, and counting their *coups* around them. Ahead of us was black darkness, heavy silence. As we went on, our hearts became more and more heavy; we feared that all of the troops had been killed.

We came to a place where the river was rippling and murmuring, as water does over a shallow stony bed, and De Rudio urged that we attempt to ford it there. I saw Girard, close beside me, take his watch out—it was a valuable gold watch—hold it aloft; and then, in Sioux, he murmured: "Oh Powerful One, Day Maker! And you, people of the depths, this I sacrifice to you. Help us, I pray you, to cross safely here!" And with that, he tossed out the watch. We heard it splash into the water. "What were you saying—what was that splash?" De Rudio asked.

"Take hold of my horse's tail, I will lead in," Girard replied. In we went, slowly, feeling our way. Nowhere across was the water up to our horses' knees! When we reached the other shore I bit my lips hard to keep from laughing; all for nothing had been Girard's sacrifice to his gods.

Here on the other shore was high grass and thick brush. We went quartering up through it, and realized eventually that we were on an island. We found ourselves facing the main channel of the river. As no shots had been fired on the opposite bluffs since nightfall, we now believed that the remnant of Reno's troops had been killed up there, and, after some talk, decided to go up where we had crossed the river after separating from Custer and Benteen, and take the back trail for Powder River.

Girard led off up the island, with De Rudio at his side, and I followed with O'Neil on the left of my horse. We had not gone more than two hundred yards, when, from a clump of brush not far ahead, a deep voice demanded in Sioux: "Who are you!"

The sudden challenge almost stunned me. I saw De Rudio and O'Neil drop down into the waist-high grass, heard Girard reply, as he checked up his horse: "Just us few."

"And where are you going?"

"Out here a way," Girard calmly answered as he turned and rode back past me, saying: "Quick! We must draw them after us!"

We rode swiftly down the island for several hundred yards, saw that we were not pursued, and stopped, then heard a few shots up where we had left De Rudio and O'Neil, and a moment later heard the splashing of horses crossing the west channel of the river, and then the thudding of their feet as they went swiftly down the flat toward the enemy camp.

"Those Indians were pickets! Reno's outfit has not been wiped out; it is still on the bluffs on the other side," I said.

"Right you are!" Girard replied.

We knew that our friends had fired the shots and frightened that group of pickets so badly that they had left the island. We did not dare return to them, lest we should reveal their hiding-place to others of the enemy; all up and down the valley the brush might be full of them. We were ourselves in great danger, crashing through the brush with our horses, and decided that, if we were ever to rejoin the troops, we should have to do it on foot. We tied our horses in a dense growth of willows, left the island, and went on up the valley. Below, the Indians were still dancing and singing victory songs around their open fires.

A little way above the head of the island, we came to a very wide reach of the river that looked as though it was fordable, and decided to try it. As we were taking off our shoes and socks and trousers, I whispered to Girard: "If you had your watch now to sacrifice it—"

"I have given it; I have faith that we shall cross," he answered.

We waded in, each carrying a stick with which we prodded ahead for quicksand or sudden drop of the bottom. On the other side we ran up into the brush, put on our clothes, and, with rifles cocked and ready, started on. Moving cautiously, we began climbing a steep brush and timber slope. We had reached a height from which, looking down the valley, we could see the many dancing fires of the enemy, when I stepped upon a dry stick that broke with a loud snap.

Close above us, a Sioux said: "Spotted Elk, did you hear that?"

"Yes. Maybe a deer," came the reply, up off to our left.

"I am thirsty; let us go down to the river," said another picket, above on our right, and at that, Girard and I turned and went leaping down the slope. I stumbled and fell over a log and crashed into a clump of rose-brush.

Below me, still another picket cried out. "What is the trouble up there?"

"Something running; sounds like a bear," one off to my left replied.

As I sat up, I could no longer hear Girard, and did not know whether he had stopped or gone back to the river. There were Sioux below me, above me, probably others scattered all along the slopes running up to the bluffs. The one who had said that he was thirsty said, "Any one going to the river with me?"

None replied. I heard him go down the slope; after a time, go back up it. Then all was silent. Weakened by lack of sleep and food, I began to doze as I sat there in the brush, surrounded though I was by the enemy. My head would nod. I would lean over more and more until about to lose my balance, then straighten up with a jerk. After a time I realized that I had slept, for I felt refreshed. I opened my eyes and saw that day was coming. All was still quiet there on the slope and down in the valley. Then, in the half-light of the coming day, a number of shots were

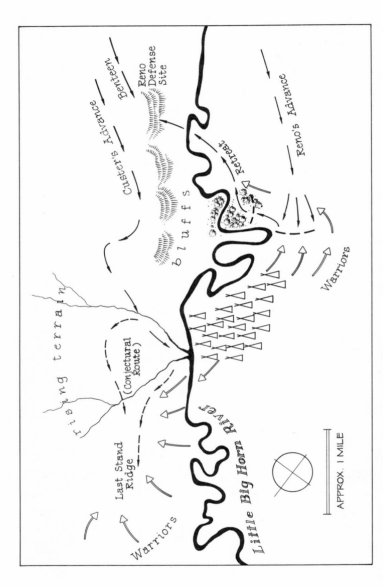

The Battle of the Little Big Horn, June 25–26, 1876.

fired below. This aroused the pickets surrounding me. One of them cried out: "There are still a few soldiers alive down there!"

"Yes. But probably those shots ended them," said another.

"Let us go down and see," one to my left proposed.

"You know that Gall told us to stay up here until he comes to make the big attack," said another.

"Well, anyhow, we can go down to our horses, and be ready to join him when he comes with his many," still another proposed.

"Yes, yes. Let us do that," the others agreed, and I heard them coming down on each side of me. I crouched still lower in my little brush corral. One of them passed within fifteen feet of me, the tail of his war bonnet fluttering behind him. As they went, a few more shots were fired, down in the valley. I may as well explain right here what was taking place down there:

When Girard and I left De Rudio and O'Neil, they remained on the island. In the dim light of dawn, they saw a large number of riders going up the valley, made out that one of them was wearing buckskin clothes, were sure that they recognized him, and De Rudio shouted: "Tom Custer! Wait!"

The answer to that was forty or fifty shots that struck all around the two, strangely enough, not one of them taking effect. They ran, dodging this way and that way around the thick clump of brush, and finally, coming to a big jam of driftwood and brush, they dropped down in it, and none came to look for them there.

This was because, just at that time, heavy firing broke out on top of the bluffs, and the party that was searching for them hurried to cross the river and join in the daylight attack upon Reno's position. The hillside pickets who had gone down past me came hurrying up on their horses and passed on each side of my brush patch as they went on to get into the fight. The firing on the day before had been terrible, but this was far heavier. I concluded that Reno and Custer and Benteen had got their troops together, and were doing the best that they could against three thousand Sioux and Cheyennes. I did not have the slightest hope that they would last an hour, so great were the odds against them.

After a time, the firing slackened, died out, and I said to myself: "That settles it; the last ones of the troops have been killed." But soon the shooting broke out again, and I knew that it wasn't the end for them. Then, as the day wore on, and I knew by the sound of the firing that successive attacks upon the troops were being repulsed, I felt that they might hold their position until General Terry, with General Gibbon and his troops, could come to aid them. This was June 26th, the day that they were due to arrive here.

The day wore on. Now and then straggling riders passed up and down near my hiding-place. Late in the afternoon, I heard a commotion below, and, at some risk of discovery, I stood up to see what it was about: a multitude of people, countless bands of horses, were going up the valley. The women and children and old men were moving camp while their warriors continued to fight up on the bluffs. I could hear, more clearly than the firing above, the shrill voices of the women as they sang. They were happy, they were singing victory songs, but still the fighting was going on. I could not understand that. Where was victory for them when the fight was not ended? I worried about it. I got up again, and looked down into the valley: there were more people, more horses in the long broad column going up the valley, than I had ever seen together. I said to myself: "Now I understand. Their warriors are so many that they know that they will wipe out the troops. They sing of the sure victory that their fighters are winning." I sank down in my hiding-place with heavy heart.

From that time I saw no more riders on the slope where I lay, and when, at nightfall, the firing entirely ceased, I decided that the last of the troops had been wiped out, and the victorious warriors had passed above me as they went to join their moving camp. Of the three men who had been with me the night before, I believed that De Rudio and O'Neil were dead, and that Girard was probably already on his way back to the Yellowstone. I decided to strike out for there, too. It would be useless for me to go out where the troops had made their last stand; I could not bury the dead, there would be no wounded for me to aid: Sioux and Cheyennes never left any wounded enemies on the field. Well, first I must have some water. I got up, stretched my numb legs, and started for the river.

Though I was quite sure that there were now no enemies on the slope, I went down it very slowly, often stopping to look and listen. I was about to kneel, and drink when, close on my left, I heard in Sioux: "Who are you?" And though I flinched, I recognized the voice. "Girard!" I cried. "Don't shoot!"

We ran to grip each other's hands. I told him my experiences, and he said that he had found a good hiding-place in an old driftwood pile overgrown with high rose-brush, and had run little risk of discovery, though many of the enemy had ridden near him. He did not believe that all of our troops had been killed up on the bluffs, as firing up there had kept up until it was too dark for any one to shoot with certainty. I proposed that we cross the river, get our horses if they were still where we had tied them, and then go up where the troops had made their stand, but he insisted that we go up from where we were; we could look for the horses later.

We found a heavy trail that the enemy had used during the day, and followed it up the slope from the river, going more and more slowly as we neared the top of the bluffs. At last we stopped side by side to look and listen;

stood there a long time, heard nothing, saw nothing. Finally, Girard whispered to me: "Well, I guess they are all dead up there."

But just then we heard a strange noise, nudged one another, listened more intently, heard it again, knew what it was: the husky, coughing groan of a horse. "Hi, there!" cried Girard.

And oh, how glad we were when we heard some one close above us, reply in good American: "Who are you?"

"Girard! Jackson! Don't shoot!" we shouted, and ran to the top and were met by my brother and a number of men of Captain Benteen's company. The first thing they asked was: "Have you seen anything of General Custer's column?"

We briefly related our experiences, and said that we were sure that Lieutenant De Rudio and Private O'Neil were dead.

Then we sat down, Girard and I, and Robert brought us hardtack, and told us of the terrible time the troops had had here on the bluffs. With knives, broken canteens, and the like, they had thrown up slight breastworks, but the enemy, shooting from higher ground, had killed some of the men where they lay behind them. Time and time again, great numbers of the enemy on horseback had all but succeeded in taking the position. There had been great suffering from want of water, and several men had been killed in going to the river for it. All would have been lost had not Benteen, and then MacDougall, joined Reno soon after he made the top of the bluffs. In the worst of the fighting, Reno, Benteen, [Captain Thomas H.] French, and all the other officers had kept going from company to company, encouraging the men, supplying them with cartridges; that they had not all been killed was a miracle.

A little way back from where we sat, men were groaning; we learned that fifty wounded men were lying there, and near them, many dead. A later count of the losses in

Reno's battalion was: killed, sixty-seven; wounded, fifty-two.

An hour or so after Girard and I rejoined our column, De Rudio and O'Neil came up, and received hearty welcome.

It was believed that the Indians would make another attack upon us, and we held ourselves ready to meet it. Day came at last. We looked down into the valley: all of the enemy had gone, taking their lodge-skins and belongings, but leaving their sets of lodge-poles standing. Away below the encampment, we saw a heavy cloud of dust rolling up the valley. Either more Indians or troops were coming. A little later, with their field-glasses, Captain French and Lieutenant Varnum made out that those advancing were troops, and shouted the good news. We watched the long column of them come on, cross the river, and go into camp where, two days before, the enemy had made the sudden and overwhelming assault upon us. Then some of the officers came up to us, General Terry, General Gibbon, and others. We were all of us happily smiling as we watched them meet our officers.

And then our smiles froze on our faces, our hearts felt as though they were lead within us, when we learned that, not far below us, they had found General Custer and all of his command, dead, stripped, and mutilated! Then I knew why, on the previous day, the women and old men of the great camp had been singing the victory song as they moved up the valley.

There on the bluffs we buried our dead as best we could. General Terry's men carried our wounded down to their camp. Girard and I went down and found our horses right where we had left them, and then we helped bury Charlie Reynolds, Bloody Knife, and others of Reno's troops.

We then went down the valley a couple of miles, recrossed the river, and came to General Custer's battlefield, a sight more terrible than I can describe. Of all the two hundred and three men in his command, he alone was not scalped or mutilated.

But it was different with the body of his brother, Captain Tom Custer: it was barely recognizable. The moment that I saw it I thought of Rain-in-the-Face's prophecy in the Fort Lincoln guard-house more than a year before. I believed that this was his work. It was, as I learned several years later. Yes, Rain-in-the-Face alone killed Captain Custer, and then cut out his heart!

While some of us were burying the dead, others were making litters for carrying the wounded. Meantime, word had been sent to the captain of the *Far West*, on the Yellowstone, to bring his boat up the Bighorn as far as he could. We all started down from the battle-field at sundown, traveling very slowly, as the wounded men had to be moved with the greatest care. At daybreak we put them aboard the *Far West*, which had come forty miles up the Bighorn.

As soon as the wounded were all on board, the *Far West* started for Fort Lincoln, more than seven hundred miles distant and arrived there after a run of only fifty-four hours.

Chapter 5
Sibley's Ordeal in the Big Horns, July 6–9, 1876
Baptiste Pourier

The first engagement between troops and Indians following the Little Big Horn was hardly a classic encounter involving tactical troop dispositions. Rather, it involved a scouting party from General Crook's camp along Big Goose Creek, where that officer had ensconced his command following his battle at Rosebud Creek on June 17. While to the north Terry and Gibbon contended with the emergency posed in the aftermath of Custer's tragedy, Crook, as yet unaware of that catastrophic event, rested his men awaiting orders and reinforcements from the south.

A principal member of the so-called Sibley Scout was Baptiste Pourier, a well-known guide and interpreter highly regarded by Crook. Born in 1841 in Saint Charles, Missouri, Pourier at age fourteen traveled to Wyoming and worked for John Richard hauling wood and caring for horses. Later he operated a mule train at Fort Fetterman, and in 1870 at Fort Laramie he signed on as an army scout. Known fondly as "Big Bat" to distinguish him from another scout, Baptiste ("Little Bat") Garnier, Pourier joined Crook's expedition early in 1876 and stayed for the duration. Respected almost universally for his abilities, Big Bat was present at many army-Sioux engagements throughout the 1860s and 1870s. In his later life he resided on the Pine Ridge Reservation in South Dakota, where he died in 1932. Pourier's account of the Sibley Scout was recorded by Eli S. Ricker in 1907. It is in Tablet 15 of the Ricker Interviews, Nebraska State Historical Society, Lincoln.

GENERAL CROOK AND HIS ARMY WAS CAMPED on the south fork of Goose Creek, about a mile above the junction of the north and south forks. Where they unite is the beginning of Tongue River. . . . Gen. Crook was contemplating employ-

Baptiste Pourier, guide and interpreter for General Crook in 1876. Courtesy of the Nebraska State Historical Society, Lincoln.

ing some Crow scouts to accompany him on his expedition north. He called Frank Gruard [Grouard] and Big Bat and told them he wanted them to go to the Crow village, and he asked them how many men they wanted to go with them & they replied they wanted 30 of the best men with good horses, and these were given them under the command of Lt. [Frederick W.] Sibley. Among these was one packer who went just as a volunteer without carrying any pack. Bat thinks he may have made 31, but is not sure . . .

They started a little before sundown—went north to a little dry creek on the north side of South Goose Cr. & which empties into Goose Cr. At this place they stopped just as the sun was going down and made a cup of coffee, & soon after this they started & arrived at Tongue River at dark and Gruard suggested to Bat that they stop there for the night. But Bat resisted this, saying that they were probably being watched by Indians who had observed their movements & were aware of their location, and that it would be better to move off a few miles since it was now dark, & thus avoid the Indians who might now know where they were. Gruard saw the reasonableness of the situation, and they moved about two miles north toward the foot of the mountains. There they found a basin about 50 yds. across, & here they camped for the night without unsaddling their horses. The men laid down to sleep and held the bridle reins of their horses in their hands.

They were up in the morning before break of day and without taking any refreshment moved forward. They had gone but half a mile when they came near a high hill with very steep sides, too sharp for horses to climb, when Gruard said to Bat, "You and the Lieut. go up to that ravine (pointing) and I will go to the top of this hill and look with the glass." Gruard left his horse at the bottom of the hill & went up. Before this, however, he told Bat that if he swung his hat that he (Bat) should at once come up to him. Bat and the Lieut. and the party moved to the head of the ravine & stopped. Presently Gruard swung his sombrero. Bat spurred his horse up to the side of Gruard's horse, dismounted and left the two horses together, & he was soon by G's side. G. said: "Take this glass and look and see if those are Indians or rocks over on that hill." Bat took the glass & looked. Then he said, "Those are Indians—a war party of Indians!" "Of course they are," said Gruard. "They are Crows, I believe." Bat replied: "I believe they are Sioux, but hold on. I can tell whether they are Sioux or Crows when they start." (They were dismounted and all in a bunch holding their horses when these scouts discovered them.) This is a rule among the Sioux and the Crows: When the Sioux are moving on the warpath or at any time they observe no regularity but pass and repass one another even the leader or head man; whereas the Crows move as our cavalry do, none ever go ahead of the leader and fall back at will.

As soon as these Indians were seen to mount, they began to pass one another without any orderly movement, at the same time dashing toward Tongue River where they expected to find the soldiers who, it was now plain, had been discovered the night before, and who, but for Bat's knowledge and judgment, would now have been attacked. There were about 50 Indians. The Indians failing to find the troops on the river had no difficulty to take their trail, which they followed up in the direction of where the soldiers now were, at the head of the ravine. The troops were now at the head of the ravine & on the top of the mountain which is in the Big Horn range. From this place the scouts had seen the Indian village 4 or 5 miles distant. The wicki-ups were standing. The command was on a big Indian trail where the natives were in the habit of going and cutting lodgepoles. Bat told the Lieut. to hurry up, for the Indians "will cut us off if we do not hurry." Gruard rode in front with the Lieut., while Bat took his place in the rear to watch from that point.

Bat was in a desperate hurry, knowing how much at this moment speed meant. He kept urging those in front to "hurry up, or the Indians will overtake us." Gruard yelled back: "We can't go any faster. The Indians haven't seen us!" The command soon filed down the hill and were in the

mountains on Tongue River in a little park. Here all
stopped. Bat said: "What are you going to do?" The Lieut.
answered: "We've got to make some coffee for these men."
Bat yelled back to Gruard: "Frank, you know better than
that. We'll be jumped sure!" Bat screamed again: "What
are you going to do? Going to take the saddles off, too?"
Lieut. said: "Yes, we are going to unsaddle." Bat answered:
"Well, my horse is going to be tied to this tree," adding
that he was not going to take the saddle off from his horse.

Coffee was made and quaffed, then the men saddled
up and started to ascend another hill. (While the coffee was
making Bat could not repress his disposition for fun-
making; so, as John F. Finerty had gone on this scout for
adventure and to enlarge his knowledge, Bat, who knew
that the Indians had accomplished their design to get ahead
of the scouts to prepare an ambuscade for them, and that
there was a warm time coming, began to rally Finerty by
saying to him that now he would have something to send to
his paper, meaning the *Chicago Times*, for which he was
correspondent. Finerty said "Yes, it was the last scout he
would accompany for the sake of news; and he hoped nothing more serious would occur than had already happened."
Bat then told him to look out for things of stirring interest
to come.) Soon they were on the top. Here Bat saw two
coup sticks which the Indians had left lying on the ground.
This was a sign which was unmistakable that the Indians
had discovered the scouts and had got ahead of them. Now
was Bat's turn to speak: "Oh, no! They did not see us! Here
are these sticks. They are ahead of us now!" These sticks
were coup sticks which had been left or dropped by the
Indians in their haste to move off into the pines, probably
when they saw troops advancing. There were fresh tracks
of their horses also. This stop for coffee had given the Indians time to get on ahead of the troops. Bat dropped back to
his place in rear and the column moved forward. (It should
be observed that at the time when they stopped for coffee

that Gruard was sick on account of a venereal disease, and when the horses were unsaddled Gruard laid down and rested on his saddle, and when they were ready to go Bat had to go and rouse him up and urge him to get his horse ready, &c.)

The sticks were seen on top of a hill. At this point it was where Bat said: "Go on ahead; I'll drop back." They moved on & were soon in the thick pines. Bat now looked back and saw three Indians coming behind. When he saw these he rode up to the Lieut. and Gruard and said to them: "They are right behind us." Bat loped on ahead and saw a lot of Indians in front looking for the trail of the troops. Bat was now right on the lead with Gruard and the Lieut. as they advanced. They were now in a park. On the right of the soldiers was a ridge covered with big rocks.

Just as the column got opposite the rocks the Indians who were hid behind the rocks rose up. Bat shouted: "Look out. They are going to fire!" Instantly the Indians began firing at a range of not more than 100 yds. The scouts broke for the pine timber on the left, not more than 20 yds away. Bat said to Frank: "Let's dismount," and the men did. Bat was the first man to act. He was about 50 yards from Gruard & the Lieut. when he dismounted. Gruard said to the Lieut. that it was necessary to dismount and tie the horses, and the Lieut. gave the order.

When the firing began the mare which John F. Finerty, the correspondent of the *Chicago Times*, rode, was wounded. This was the only damage done. The men hid in the brush and behind rocks and trees. The Indians kept their places behind the rocks and did not cease firing, and reinforcements were eventually arriving, and the Indian fire steadily increased in volume. When the troops took their present position in the timber it must have been two or three o'clock in the afternoon. . . . Bat thinks they were here several hours. He is sure it must have been close to night when they stole away.

Bat was studying the situation all the while that the troops were lying in the woods without firing. The soldiers remained doggedly silent—not a voice was heard—not the crack of a gun on their side. (Once during this one-sided conflict an Indian named Painted Horse [who is living now (1907) on White Clay Creek on Pine Ridge Reservation] called out: "O Bat! Come over here. I want to tell you something. Come over!" This he repeated, but Bat knew too well that this was no time for friendly converse, and that it was only a ruse to ascertain whether he was in the party, and if he was to gain some advantage over him, if it be only to put him out of the way. For Bat was well known to these Indians, and they realized that he was a shrewd and energetic antagonist. [It has been published that this call was made to Gruard. This is fiction.]) Bat reasoned that they could not hold out indefinitely. They were not more than seven miles from the Indian village they had seen in the morning. This was a Sioux and Cheyenne village. He knew that their position was untenable—that the Indians were hourly increasing in numbers and that they would in time be numerous enough to surround them; he saw that the pine leaves and cones and the decaying brush and trees and the dead limbs which were thick on the ground would make a terrible holocaust when the time should come when the cunning Indians would apply the match to these highly inflamable materials. When that time should come, as it was sure to, the troops would be in a roaring furnace. The end would be there. No man would escape incineration. If he should attempt it the foxy Indians would see him and he would fall before their rifles like wild prey. There would be no hope and no escape. The only chance for safety was in prompt and early action. Bat was reasoning it out all alone as he sat behind that large pine tree cogitating, where he had already escaped a wound in his knee by the timely withdrawing of his leg a moment before the missile swept down a twig within his reach. Bat said to himself, "This horse I ride is my own. To stay here is to die soon and miserably. I can leave the horse—he will be sacrificed at all events—and there will be some chance for me to get away. The only sensible thing to do is to take that chance and make the most of it. What is good for me in this respect will be equally good for all the others. It is my duty to save this command." So reasoning, his resolution was quickly formed. He was lying in the extreme front on the right and Lieutenant Sibley, Frank Gruard and John F. Finerty were on the left. Crawling on his belly to where these men lay, Bat said to the Lieutenant: "What are you going to do?" The officer replied: "There is nothing to do. We can't do anything." Bat said: "We can do something. Let's leave our horses tied and get out of here. I've got my horse tied; he is my own private property, and he will stay there. If you were wounded, Lieutenant, we would pull out and leave you; if I was wounded, you would pull out and leave me. Therefore, let us leave our horses and get out of here before any of us are wounded." The Lieutenant said: "That is all we can do. Go and tell Frank about it."

Bat now crawled in the same manner to where Gruard lay a little farther to the left. He said to Gruard: "Frank, let's get out of here," and he explained his view of the matter over again. Gruard replied, "That is the only show we've got." While Bat and Gruard were talking, a Cheyenne Indian costumed in a gaudy war-bonnet . . . had been cantering up and down in the open space between the troops and the Indians offering a challenge to the scouts to fire so they might betray their places of concealment. Gruard said to Bat, "Let's get ready and shoot that Indian when he comes again." The two men brought their pieces into position for use. When he was opposite of them they both fired and the bold rider fell to the ground dead. These were the only shots fired by the scouts during their stay in this position.

Lieut. Sibley was a young man just out of West Point,

about medium height, spare as young men usually are; of handsome features, fine figure, intelligent, gentlemanly, refined, brave, and at all times as cool as if on dress parade. If he had not been a man of sound practical common sense, and taken the advice of the rough frontiersmen who were sent to guide and serve him, he would have lost his command and his own life.

Having dispatched the saucy Indian, Bat now renewed his urging on Gruard for immediate action. He said: "Now hurry up, Frank, let's get out of here. Let's go to the Lieut., and let's get out of here." Both then crawled to Lt. Sibley, who spoke up when they had reached him, and said: "Frank, what will we do?" Gruard replied: "What Bat told you. It is all we can do." The Lieutenant gave the command to the men which was passed along from man to man, to get their ammunition from their horses, concealing themselves as much as possible while doing so, and to assemble on the left, so that the whole party might withdraw in a body without straggling. This was done in a few minutes' time. Bat said to Gruard, "You go ahead and I will go behind and see that all keep up."

All moved out as noiselessly as could be. The Indian fire did not slacken. The horses were behind to keep up the delusion among the enemy that the scouts were still in their old position, and these poor animals were painful targets for bullets. Some of them were groaning with pain from wounds when the men secretly withdrew. The men had gone but a short distance when they emerged into a glade, miniature in size. A few steps, and they were beyond it and into a motley forest wherein fire had once done havoc, and the leaning dead trees, which were held up by the living ones, marked every possible angle and interlaced the standing timber, while the ground was strewn with blackened trunks and limbs, the whole forming an entanglement which required the utmost patience and labor on the part of the fugitives to overcome, and ren-

Second Lieutenant Frederick W. Sibley, Second U.S. Cavalry, who commanded Crook's scouting detachment during its post–Little Big Horn encounter with the Indians. Courtesy of Jerome A. Greene.

dered their progress most difficult and slow. They toiled on until they came to Tongue river, when they had to cross on a fallen tree which spanned the stream. (Bat kept advising the men to step on the stones and not on the soil, so they would leave no trail for the Indians to follow; and sometimes this advice was communicated in Bat's nervous, energetic and explosive style of speech, which could not be heard without leaving an impressive effect for immediate good to all.) The Lieutenant, who was in the lead just behind Gruard, had a mishap in making the passage over. He slipped and went into the water, and the men had to fish him out.

It was now dusky from nightfall, and the ascent of the Big H. mountain was begun. When the top was attained, night had fully settled down. The men had had nothing to eat since the day before; they had just a cup of coffee before their encounter with the Indians. Now hunger was oppressing them. The excitements of the day and the strain of care and exertion had told on their strength and they were nigh exhaustion.

The men halted to rest and soon sleep had disarmed almost all of them of the slightest concern. The scouts had only light clothing, and Bat had not even his blouse, for this had been left behind on his horse. So he started a fire under an overhanging ledge of rock; but while he was doing this the sergeant came to him and remarked that he should not kindle a fire, that it was against orders and was dangerous as it would show to the Indians where they were. But Bat adhered to his purpose, saying that it would do no harm, and, moreover, he would rather be killed by a bullet than by frost, and with an expletive as strong as his proper determination, the interview closed between the two, when the sergeant said he would have to rouse the Lieutenant and let him know, and Bat said, "Go and tell him; I am going to have a fire."

The Lieutenant came forward and in his accustomed

kindly way asked Bat if he did not think it was dangerous to have a fire. Bat said, "No. Look at this rock above us and the timber all around us. The Indians cannot see this little fire. Besides, I am cold and must be warmed." Sibley said: "All right, Bat. I am awfully cold myself," and being soaked from his immersion in the river below, he hovered close to the little blaze which Bat had so firmly produced and spread his arms out over it, and in a little while was feeling much better.

Another circumstance went far toward making this fire a wonderfully grateful source of satisfaction to the tired men. Snow and rain were falling in about equal proportions. It was dark as pitch. There was no moon and the clouds were dense and ominous. It was but a few minutes till all the men were crowding around to receive the welcome warmth. Gruard crawled off and sought rest lying up against the granite wall. The men overcame their shivering and they threw themselves down upon the ground to drown their consciousness in slumber. A guard was kept in proximity to the campfire during the night, and was changed at regular intervals so that there was not a man who did not become refreshed with sleep and relaxation.

When daylight came the party resumed their perilous journey toward Gen. Crook's camp. They had gone a few miles, probably six or eight, when as they were trailing a small wild game path at the summit of the mountain they came into a spot where the timber was light and thin, and Bat discovered a war party of thirty-two (32) Indians trailing along at the base of the mountain. He informed Gruard, who was now in the rear, it being difficult for him to keep up, owing to his disability, Bat being the active guide in the lead. Gruard said that as these Indians were ahead of the scouts and going in the direction of their camp, it would be necessary for the scouts to fall back into the woods and keep themselves concealed during the day from discovery by the enemy. They retreated a hundred yards or so and laid down under the pines and waited for night. (Here the men, because their strength was now overtaxed, lightened their loads by depositing some 250 rounds of ammunition under a stone and left it there.) The weather was clear and warm and the shade was as welcome as the fire had been only a few hours before. The men were hungry and sore. Every now and then some one of the luckless scouts would voice his cravings in expressions like this: "Oh! If I only had something to eat I would be all right!"

(This party of Indians that had been seen on the flank of the mountain at the foot went on to spy about Crook's camp and steal and drive off any livestock that they could get. They got two saddle horses which belonged to Bat & were left at the camp when he started on the scout. They took 3 or 4 head of horses besides—some that belonged to some miners who were with the expedition. These Indians started fires to burn Crook out, but they failed in the design.)

While lying in the pines this day Bat enraged Finerty again when he said to him: "You will have lots to send to your paper when you get back to camp." In his position this was irritating, especially as no man in the party could be supposed to cherish at this stage of the war-game the most amiable feelings. Finerty remarked once more: "I'll never go out on a scout again for news. Damn you, Bat, you are always making fun of me!" Finerty wore a very large boot that turned up at the toe like a prairie schooner at either end. This was an unfortunate design of the Irish shoemaker, for the correspondent on this occasion, as it was continually hooking the brush and grasses and causing him to fall, which was a trying annoyance.

When the darkness of night came the march began again. It took about eight miles' travel to bring them to middle Goose Creek, but in journeying this distance Bat had his hands full to keep Gruard moving. Twice before they got to this stream he had to go back to rouse him up and get him on his feet and to encourage him with pleas and drive him by cursings to maintain his place in the column and not oblige the column to wait for him. He protested that he was sick and distressed and without strength, but took Bat's urgings and imprecations in the best of good spirit, for he was a good-natured man and felt that Bat had nothing but his welfare at heart, and then he would renew his promises to do the best he could.

When they had come to the stream the men severally made their choice whether they would strip themselves of clothing and carry it in a bundle above their heads, or whether they would wear their clothes while wading through, and have to suffer with them wet when they were over. While going across two of the men slipped on stones and lost their guns. Others slipped in the same way and fell in the water and got their clothing that they were carrying well soaked. The water, of course, being from the melting snow on the mountains, was desperately cold. At this place one of the men who had thrown away his shoes before they had arrived at the place where they rested all day, and whose feet were terribly swollen from wounds by prickly pears and sharp stones, was so disheartened and indifferent to his safety that he refused to cross the creek and follow the party farther. And he stepped aside and laid down in the thick bushes to welcome fate, be it what it might—rescue by fresh soldiers, or destruction at the hands of the enemy.

The passage of the stream having been accomplished, Bat started another fire, but not without a query from the Lieutenant as to the safety of the proceeding. But being assured by the scout who thought if there was any danger, which he did not believe, it was better to take the chances than to suffer from cold and still farther weaken and debilitate the men, that there was not a particle of danger, and so the fire was made and the men dried and warmed, and the result justified Bat's judgment.

After the men had become comfortable the march continued, but it could not be kept up steadily, but every mile or two they halted to rest; and so the night passed away marching and resting by turns till morning dawned. The sun rose clear and warm and shed its bright beams down on the straggling party of men who were lame and weak, and faint in body but strong of purpose, whose stomachs were empty and whose eyes had a strange unnatural look. Constantly they turned their heads looking in all directions; this was a precaution which the first law of nature enforced by instinct, for no prescience could give warning of the moment when a party of the enemy would burst upon them from some quarter and "rush" them to instant death.

Bat explains here that the Indians watch from high places. They can tell if any persons are in the vicinity if they see the wild game running. He used always to observe this sign: if men "wind" the game (that is, get on the windward side) the animals take the scent and flee. So the Indians act intelligently and surely by this sign, and in dangerous times men move in the Indian country in momentary liability of being discovered and attacked by the redskins.

It was sometime this morning that Bat saw Lieutenant Sibley seize a little bird that was hopping in the grass and devour it. He remarked to the officer: "That is pretty rough, Lieutenant." "Yes, Bat," replied the starving man, "but I am so hungry that I do not know what to do!" Afterwards he saw a soldier do the same thing. How many more surrendered to their ravenous appetites in a similar way he does not know. But for himself he says that he had been going alone that morning uprooting with his hunting knife an occasional Indian turnip that he found, and eating it, and though it gave but little nourishment, it contributed something to sustain him in his weakness. (How aggravating to these famished men it was to see wild game sporting in the air and on the plains, and yet they dare not shoot from fear that the report of firearms would attract the Indians and lead to their own certain destruction.)

About the middle of the forenoon joyful evidence of rescue appeared. A mule belonging to the pack train [of Crook's command] had disappeared, and Dave Mears, the assistant chief packer, had gone out a mile or more to see if he could get any trace of it. In the distance he saw a man, but, supposing he was an Indian, he did not advance toward him, but waited and watched his movements. When the man saw him he made signs which were unintelligible, and kept on coming toward Mr. Mears, who remained in the one position till he was convinced that it was not an Indian but a white man in distress, when he went toward him till they met, and he learned from this abject man the situation and whereabouts of the returning scouts. Uncle Dave went back to the camp with the information, and men were speedily sent to their assistance. The first to reach them was a packer riding a mule. Then horses came for all the men to ride into camp, which was now in sight. . . . A company of cavalry was sent out on the trail of the scouts to recover the man who had been left behind on the opposite bank of the Middle Goose, and he was found and brought into camp.

Chapter 6
The Skirmish at Warbonnet Creek, July 17, 1876
Charles King

Within weeks of the Custer disaster the army sent reinforcements afield. Colonel Wesley Merritt with the Fifth U.S. Cavalry was ordered north to bolster Crook's flagging command in the wake of that officer's encounter at Rosebud Creek. While Crook camped along Big Goose Creek in northern Wyoming, Merritt's troopers scouted northeast of Fort Laramie into the Nebraska panhandle, where on July 17 they encountered a large party of Cheyenne warriors setting out from nearby Red Cloud Agency to join the so-called hostiles in Montana. It was the first meeting between a major army command and the Indians after Little Big Horn.

First Lieutenant Charles King was a participant in the fight at Warbonnet Creek. An 1866 graduate of West Point, King served most of his army career on the frontier fighting Indians in the Southwest and on the Northern Plains. In 1874 he was wounded in a skirmish with Apaches in Arizona; three years after his Sioux War service the effects of that lingering injury forced his retirement from the army. Although he saw brief service with volunteer troops during the Spanish-American War, King settled into a life of letters, becoming the prolific author of some seventy books based on his military experiences. He died in 1933, one of the last surviving officers of the Great Sioux War. King's essay about the Warbonnet fight was published in the Denver Post *on March 10, 1914.*

IT WAS THE CENTENNIAL SUMMER, and the eyes of the nation seemed focused on Philadelphia. Every art and industry was there represented, and to further attract the array of sightseers from all over the land, "shows" without number had pre-empted every suitable hall or theater in

First Lieutenant Charles King, Fifth U.S. Cavalry, regimental adjutant during the Big Horn and Yellowstone expedition. Courtesy of Paul L. Hedren.

the neighboring cities. And yet, at the very outset of what promised to be a very profitable season, one theatrical company doing a rushing business summarily disbanded. It was "Buffalo Bill's Own," then playing to crowded houses, and the simple explanation of it all was that the papers had just announced a serious Indian war in the West, and that the Fifth regiment of cavalry had been ordered from the southern plains to hasten to the support of Gen. George Crook's column in Wyoming. This was the regiment which, six and seven years earlier, [William F.] Cody had guided as chief scout on the campaign against Tall Bull and the Southern Cheyennes, and now their old comrade could not bear the idea of their again going campaigning without him.

The wires had flashed his message to Cheyenne within the hour after he read the news. The wires flashed back to him the answer from the regiment:

"Your old position open to you. Join us here." And for four days thereafter he was eagerly welcomed by every officer and man, as much at home among them as though they had never known a day apart.

One week thereafter, under the orders of General Sheridan, they had forded the North Platte and launched out into the broad lands of the Sioux, ordered to find the route by which the young warriors were quitting the reservations of Red Cloud and Spotted Tail in northwestern Nebraska, and riding away laden with rations, arms and ammunition, to join the great herds of "hostiles" under the renowned medicine chief, Sitting Bull—Tatonka Eyo Tonka. Their rendezvous was in the heart of the glorious country between the Big Horn range and the Yellowstone. Three columns, commanded respectively by Generals Terry, Crook and Gibbon, were closing in upon them from east, south and west. With Terry rode the famous cavalry leader of the Civil War, George Armstrong Custer. Hurrying to join Crook, and assigned to the command of the Fifth cavalry, came [Colonel] Wesley Merritt, famous even as Custer, and between those three slowly concentrating columns lurked the bands of Sitting Bull, wearily watching every move and waiting a chance to strike. On the 17th of June they swarmed on Crook's force among the bluffs of the Rosebud and brought him to a stand. On the 25th they overwhelmed Custer and his command on the banks of the Little Horn, and though Indians far and wide speedily heard of that bloody victory, not until ten days thereafter was it told to awe-stricken crowds at the Centennial. Then, people along the Delaware began to see why Buffalo Bill had closed his show, turned his back on crowded houses and box receipts, and had hastened to bear his part in the deadly and dramatic work on the frontier.

On July 1st Merritt reached the Fifth cavalry away out on the dry fork of the South Cheyenne. On the 2nd, with Buffalo Bill leading, they had their first lively chase after a war party of Sioux, and followed it with five long days of scouting under hot suns, and short nights of sleeping under the stars. Then—just as they were saddling on the morning of the 7th of July, came dread and direful news: Custer—"The Long Haired"—the daring and dashing leader, with five of his favorite companies, had been swept from the face of the earth in fierce battle with the Sioux.

Perhaps no man felt it more than Cody, who had ridden with Custer on many a run for buffalo. Perhaps no man more eagerly welcomed the news that now the regiment would be recalled to Fort Laramie to fit out with supplies, and then march to strengthen Crook's command, now in its entrenched camp at the base of the Big Horn[s]. Perhaps no man more delightedly heard Merritt's sudden order—a few days later—to face again northward, ride like the wind and be ready to fight like the devil. Eight hundred Southern [Northern] Cheyennes, old antagonists of the Fifth, had had a grand pow-wow at the Red Cloud agency, and openly declared their intention of starting to join forces with their victorious brethren under Sitting Bull.

Merritt's generalship always was fine; this day it was great. With just seven companies he was in bivouac at the moment close to Rawhide Ford of the Red Cloud–Laramie road, sixty-five miles southeast of the reservation. It was just noon, Saturday, the 15th. He had promptly reasoned that the Indians would take the broad trail across the valley of the South Cheyenne, where the Fifth had been scouting and chasing until Sheridan's order of recall reached them on the 12th. The route was now open. There was nothing to hinder the Indian move. If, as announced, they started on Sunday, they should be crossing by Monday morning. Merritt's resolve was taken instantly. He would make a wide circuit back by Rawhide Butte and Cardinal's Chair, march eighty-five miles night and day and get there first. Then—with only 400 men all told, throw himself across the Indian path, and though they might be two to his one— drive them back to the reservation.

The Indians to reach it had only an easy Sunday ride of twenty-eight miles northwestward from their abandoned camps. The Fifth cavalry, after a thirty-five-mile jog all Saturday afternoon and evening, had still a fifty-mile stage to cover, and had to make it unsuspected and unseen. With only an hour's rest at the old stockade on Sage creek, where every belt and pocket was crammed with ball cartridges, Merritt marched his hardy column, Cody and his scouts well in the lead and far out on the eastward flank, and just at 8 P.M. on Sunday, silently under the stars, halted below the bluffs of a tributary of the South Cheyenne, long known to the Indians as War Bonnet creek. Here close at hand was the grand crossing, and the Fifth had won the race. Half an hour's scout enabled Cody to assure Merritt that the hostiles were still to the southeast, between them and the

Colonel Wesley Merritt, Fifth U.S. Cavalry, who oversaw the
action at Warbonnet Creek. Courtesy of Historical Collections/
University Archives, University of Colorado at Boulder Libraries.

reservation—that it was a safe bet they would be along early Monday morning, and probably not before.

That night, in spite of yelping coyotes on every side, every horse and man, save only the watchful guard, had at least a few hours of sleep. Then came the dawn of a most eventful day—Monday, July 17th.

As the stars began to pale in the eastern sky and a faint gray light to steal over the landscape, the outlying sentries began peering over the banks and ridges behind which they were crouching. The southeast—the direction from which the hostiles should come—was the important front, and the officer of the guard, Lieutenant King, taking with him Sergeant [Edmund] Schreiber and Corporal [Thomas W.] Wilkinson, crept further out to a little knoll from which they found unobstructed view. East—southeast— south and southwest—the rolling prairie lay spread before them. Directly in their front was a broad open "swale," ris- ing gradually to a long ridge stretching from east to west. Winding away to the southwest and a little distance to their right, lay the road by which they had come the previous evening. Directly southward, with its branches cutting into the ridge, a dry water course in a shallow ravine, extended well across the swale and passing to the right of the knoll, wound its way through the bluffs to the bed of the War Bonnet. The road crossed it but a stone's throw to the right of the knoll. The ground rose in a V-shaped tongue be- tween the ravine and the road, hiding one from the other. Even as the officer, kneeling near the crest, was studying with his binocular the distant winding of the road, he was suddenly accosted by Corporal Wilkinson:

"Look, lieutenant: there are Indians!"

Levelling his glass in the direction pointed, Lieuten- ant King quickly sighted not one, but two or three groups of mounted warriors scurrying about along that southward ridge, evidently in great excitement. In a moment a mes- senger was hurried back to notify General Merritt, and

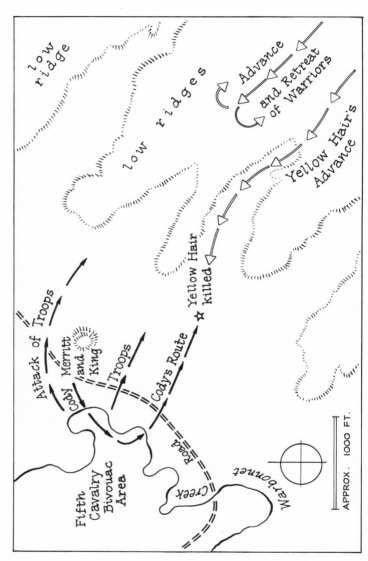

low ridge

low ridges

Advance and Retreat of Warriors

Yellow Hair's Advance

Attack of Troops

Merritt and King

Troops

Cody

Yellow Hair killed

Cody's Route

Fifth Cavalry Bivouac Area

Road

Creek

Warbonnet

APPROX. 1000 FT.

The Skirmish at Warbonnet Creek, July 17, 1876.

almost instantly this order was sent noiselessly from troop to troop:

"Saddle up and mount."

In five minutes, riding up from the hidden bivouac, came the general, with three of his staff and Buffalo Bill. Dismounting behind the knoll, they crawled up to where King kept watch. Following in a moment more came two of Cody's scouts, Tait and "Chips"—and perhaps half a dozen of the guard, all concealed behind the knoll.

Briefly, Lieutenant King pointed out the lay of the land. "What puzzles me," said he, "is the action of the Indians. There are hundreds of them along that ridge, all darting about as though watching something out on the Sage creek road, keeping hid from the west, but evidently seeing and suspecting nothing in this direction."

By this time, though the sun was not yet peeping above the horizon, every moving object along the southward ridge was distinctly visible, and the long stretch of winding road could be seen full four miles away. By this time, too, the ridge and every slope screened from the west were fairly alive with Indians, and even Cody was mystified.

"What in thunder are those fellows fooling about?" said he.

Then all of a sudden came the explanation. Afar out over the westward slopes, where the land was higher—first one, then another white dot came slowly into view until presently a little string was crawling toward them.

"The wagon train, by all that's wonderful!" cried Bill, "and we never thought they could make it!"

Make it—they had. Though expected to halt at the Sage creek stockade, Lieutenant [William P.] Hall, the quartermaster in charge, had baited his mules, piled a lot of infantrymen with their long rifles on top of his rations but under the wagon covers, and shoved ahead on an all-night march. This then, was the cause of the tremendous excitement among the Cheyennes—a rich train bound for the Black Hills! What better prize could they hope for? Already they were signalling belated brethren up from the rear, little dreaming how very much more those wagons might hold! And then suddenly, just as the sun came peering over the eastward hills, a new excitement arose. To the amaze of Merritt's party on the knoll, a brilliant little band of warriors, detaching from the main body on the ridge, came lashing full speed down the slope directly toward them, war bonnets streaming in the wind, their ponies bounding over the turf, and then, almost as suddenly came the explanation. Only a mile away to the southwest, popping suddenly over a wave of prairie, two couriers rode suddenly into view. Bearing dispatches to Merritt, believing him now so near and the coast entirely clear, they had ventured forward from the train and all unconscious of danger, were speeding straight to their death.

Like a whirlwind came the Indians—by this time speeding down the tortuous ravine, and Cody saw the scheme at a glance—to dash six to one upon the unwary riders, at the point where the road in [and] the ravine met—and the rest—could better be imagined than described.

"By Jove, general," he cried, "now's our chance! Let us mount and cut those fellows off!"

Instantly came Merritt's answer. "Up to you, Cody! Stay there, King! Watch till they're close under you, then give the word!"

It was a thrilling moment. Already six companies had saddled and ridden into line close under the screening bluffs, 200 yards to the rear—a sweet surprise would that be for the Cheyennes! Already the ridge to the south was fairly bristling with feathered crests, lances and shields, as scores of Indians watched with eager envy the dash of their fellows on the helpless prey. Already Cody, "Chips," Tait and half a dozen troopers had sprung to saddle behind the knoll. Merritt and his aids crouched half way down the slope. Only Lieutenant King remained at the crest, stretched at full length, the top of his hatless head alone visible from the Indian side. Already above the swift beating of their hearts the little party could hear the swifter tattoo of nimble hoofs upon the resounding turf. All eyes were fixed on King, awaiting his signal. Ten seconds too soon and the dashing foemen could easily veer and escape. Two seconds too late and the couriers were dead men. Presently the watchers saw the gauntleted hand cautiously lifting, higher and higher. Ten—five seconds more—and then came the ringing order:

"Now lads—in with you!"

And with an instant rush and cheer the little party of scouts and troopers burst from their concealment, tore headlong around the shoulder of [the] bluff and straight at the face of the astonished foe—Buffalo Bill ten lengths in the lead.

In the moment that followed, Merritt and his officers sprang again to the crest. The officers had only their revolvers, but Corporal Wilkinson's carbine let drive the first shot. Cool and daring the Indian leader bent low over his pony's neck and sent his answering shot close to the general's cheek, and then as he straightened in saddle, he was suddenly aware of a foeman equally daring, dashing straight upon him, half a dozen cheering troopers at his heels. One glance was more than enough. Even Indians who never before had seen him—well knew Buffalo Bill, and the lean brown arm with its glistening bracelets and brandishing lance, was thrown on high in warning to his fellows. The lance was flung aside even as, veering to the right to avoid the shock of the charge and bring his rifle into action, the superb young chief flung himself along his pony's outstretched neck to aim beneath it, just as Cody's first bullet tore through his left leg and into the gallant pony's heart, tumbling steed and rider headlong in confused and kicking heap. Frantic with excitement, his amazed followers circled to right and left, and with the young brave struggling to his feet—his rifle hurled from his grasp—his tomahawk brandished for close combat, was flung again to earth as Cody's charger stumbled over the dying pony. The next instant white chief and red—Buffalo Bill for the scouts and the cavalry—Yellow Hand [Yellow Hair] for the Southern Cheyennes, once more faced each other in deadly grapple, and in another the pride of the warrior tribe lay gasping on the sod.

Even then in the moment of his breathless victory, there was peril for Buffalo Bill. Astonished though they were at the sight of this onslaught of a handful of foes, the Cheyennes along the mile-away ridge were quick to realize what had happened, and in one magnificent dash they came charging down to the rescue. One minute the broad, sun-lit slope was fairly alive with mounted warriors, full twenty score, all full panoplied in Indian fashion, lurid with paint, brilliant with flashing ornaments, their wild war bonnets streaming behind them. On they came, yelling hate, vengeance, death and defiance, and for the moment it looked as though Cody and his little band would be swallowed up in the rush. Only for a moment though, for before half the distance from ridge to knoll had been covered, up from the screen of bluffs to the north came line after line, troop after troop of blue-shirted riders, their guidons flashing, their carbines unslung and advanced, and in a burst of cheers and a thunder of hoofs, the Fifth cavalry swooped down at the gallop. The sight was too much even for Cheyenne nerves, and, leaving their dead on the field, the bewildered, out-generaled warriors reined in, whirled about, turned and fled—never stopping until safe within the limits of the reservation, where—no matter what their sins, they were safe from soldier hands. Thither followed the Fifth—and there that night, awe-stricken Indians crept about their bivouac fires, intent on seeing the chief who had beaten them at their own game, and with fear, hatred and baffled vengeance in their eyes, following and studying the famous scout who that day had stripped them of their daring leader—Yellow Hand. In all Merritt's hard-riding column, there was no man who did not accord the honors of the day to Buffalo Bill.

Chapter 7
The Skirmish at Powder River, August 2, 1876
Orlando H. Moore

In the aftermath of the Little Big Horn defeat, General Terry and Colonel Gibbon buried Custer's men and consolidated their remaining force along the Yellowstone River to await reinforcements. By the first week in August troops of the Fifth and Twenty-second infantry regiments had reached the region commanded, respectively, by Colonel Nelson A. Miles and Lieutenant Colonel Elwell S. Otis. Terry planned to join forces with Crook, now moving north from Wyoming with Merritt's cavalry, and to scour the Yellowstone country for the Sioux and Cheyennes.

The first engagement of Terry's command with the Indians came on August 2, 1876, when Major Orlando H. Moore led a combined force of Sixth and Seventeenth infantrymen down the Yellowstone to retrieve a supply of forage that had been left at an old depot site near the mouth of Powder River. A career officer, Moore possessed twenty years' service in 1876. The native Pennsylvanian saw duty in California before the Civil War, and in that conflict he commanded Michigan troops. Moore fought at Shiloh, Corinth, Nashville, and Franklin, Tennessee, emerging from the war a colonel of volunteers. Commissioned a major in the Sixth Infantry in 1874, Moore served in the departments of Dakota and the Platte until his retirement ten years later. In his report of August 4, 1876, he detailed his fight with the tribesmen at the mouth of the Powder. The account was published in Report of the Secretary of War, 1876.

I LEFT THE MOUTH OF THE ROSEBUD AUGUST 1, 1876, at 3 P.M., on board the steamer *Far West*. My force consisted of Companies D, Captain [Daniel H.] Murdock, and I, Lieut. George B. Walker, Sixth Infantry; Company C, Captain [Malcolm] McArthur and Lieutenant [Frank D.]

Major Orlando H. Moore, Sixth U.S. Infantry, as he appeared during the Civil War. Courtesy of the U.S. Army Military History Institute.

Garretty, Seventeenth Infantry; three scouts—Messrs. [Wesley] Brockmeyer, [George W.] Morgan, and [Vic] Smith; one Napoleon and one Gatling gun, commanded by Lieut. C. A. Woodruff, Seventh Infantry.

I reached Powder River early on the morning of August 2d, and passed on down the Yellowstone around the bend to Wolf Rapids, in order to better discover and attack Indians. None could be seen, although numerous fires indicated their presence in the vicinity. I then moved to the landing where the forage had been stored, and a large quantity of oats was found with nearly all the sacks removed by the Indians, and at once made preparations to take the grain on board. The ground near the landing, on account of a circular ridge, made a strong military position, which I at once occupied. In a few minutes, some of the Indians made their appearance. I at once made a disposition of my forces for a fight, leaving ten men on board to guard the steamer.

The larger portion of my command was carefully concealed from the view of the Indians, in the hope that they would advance to an attack upon the infantry. This, however, they declined to do. I then concluded to treat them with something new, and accordingly placed Lieutenant Woodruff's artillery in position, and opened fire upon a party on our right—toward Powder River—with spherical-case shell from our 12-pounder Napoleon gun, which spread consternation among them, and they were driven all along from the ravines and fled to the bluffs, as the shells went on their exploring expeditions, bearing more to the left each successive shot, until the whole ground in the bend between Powder River and Wolf Rapids on our left was commanded by our artillery. We then went to work loading the oats.

At about 11 o'clock more Indians made their appearance on the flank near Wolf Rapids, and were repulsed by the artillery. About 1 o'clock Mr. [David] Campbell, pilot on the boat, and the scouts Brockmeyer and Morgan rode out down the river and near the bluffs, when skirmishers reported that Indians were attempting to cut them off. I discovered about twenty Indians maneuvering for this purpose, who were concealed from the view of the scouts. At this moment a well-directed shot from the Napoleon gun apprised the scouts of their danger, and defeated the movements of all but a small party of Indians, who were in advance, and who opened fire on the scouts, in which Brockmeyer and his horse fell. The scout, mortally wounded, was cared for on the spot by the gallant Dr. [Henry] Porter.

The Indian who shot Brockmeyer fell under the fire of the other scout; and the remainder of the Indians fled to the hills under the continued fire of the artillery, while Lieutenant Garretty was promptly hastening on to aid the scouts with a detachment ordered from the left flank of the line of infantry.

While this was going on some Indians were seen at Powder River Bluffs on our right. After this diversion, near dark, we completed loading the grain, which was estimated at about seventy-five tons. Nothing more being seen of the Indians, I returned with the command to the Rosebud.

The entire command deserve commendation for their energy and concord in the discharge of every duty at Powder River, including the officers of the steamer *Far West*.

Chapter 8

The Starvation March and the Battle of Slim Buttes, September 9, 1876

Bennett A. Clements and Anson Mills

On August 10, Generals Crook and Terry joined forces. They roamed fruitlessly through the Rosebud–Powder River region with nearly four thousand men—so large a command that its maneuvering was ponderous at best and its components incapable of responding efficiently if Indians appeared. One officer suggested that the command "would never catch, kill or scare 40 Indians," and dissidence appeared in the ranks of the tired soldiers. Finally, on August 25, Crook broke away and headed east, ostensibly to position his men to protect settlements in the Black Hills; in reality, he wanted to be free from Terry's control. Over the ensuing weeks Crook led his men in a grueling march through badlands and mud plains under terrible weather conditions. It rained ceaselessly. Rations gave out, and Crook ordered his men to shoot and eat the jaded cavalry mounts. The travail was interrupted by a signal encounter with the Indians at Slim Buttes, Dakota Territory—the army's first Sioux War victory.

In this selection, Bennett A. Clements offers the unique perspective of a medical officer on Crook's "Horsemeat March" and the ensuing fight at Slim Buttes, while Anson Mills recounts the role of his command in attacking the Indian village. Clements was born in the District of Columbia. Appointed first lieutenant and assistant surgeon in the army in 1856, he served in Florida, Texas, and New Mexico until July, 1862, when he transferred east as a captain. Clements was promoted to surgeon with the grade of major in 1863. He administered several hospitals during and after the Civil War and received a brevet of lieutenant colonel for faithful and meritorious service in that conflict. In 1867, Clements transferred to Jackson Barracks at New Orleans, serving there until his assignment to headquarters, Department of the Platte, at Omaha. He died while still in the army on November 1, 1886.

Anson Mills, from Indiana and Texas, dropped out of West

Point in the 1850s but won a commission in the regulars after the outbreak of the Civil War. He earned several brevet promotions during the war for meritorious service in Tennessee and Georgia. Mills transferred to the Third Cavalry in 1870 and eventually saw duty as major of the all-black Tenth Cavalry. He returned to the Third as colonel in 1892 and retired as a brigadier general five years later. Mills devised, patented, and manufactured a unique woven web cartridge belt for army use, continuing its production during part of his retirement. He died in 1924.

Clements filed the following report (abbreviated here) on December 14, 1876, after Crook's summer operation had been concluded. The original reposes in the National Archives, Record Group 94, Records of the Adjutant General's Office.

I REPORTED TO BRIGADIER GENERAL CROOK, commanding the [Big Horn and Yellowstone] expedition, on the evening of August 3, 1876, at Goose Creek, near the Big Horn mountains, and on the following day was assigned in orders as medical director of the expedition. . . .

The supplies taken consisted mainly of surgical dressings, plaster of Paris, a complete medical chest, and additional quantities of the more commonly used medicines, with a limited supply of stimulants, and they were all carried on two pack mules. In addition, twenty canvas bottoms for mule litters were carried, and it was attempted also to carry some poles for litters, but they had to be abandoned on the first day's march. The dressings and medicines were about equally distributed in two parts, one for each mule, and each medical officer carried on his horse or person a small quantity of medicines and dressings. An examination was made of all the sick and disabled of the command, of whom sixteen were designated to remain with the [supply] train, and Acting Assistant Surgeons [R. B.] Grimes and [William C.] Lecompte detailed to the charge of them. One hospital tent fly was taken, and six medical officers in all accompanied the column.

The command consisted of about 1500 cavalry, 450 infantry, 45 white "volunteers," and 240 Snake and Ute

Surgeon Bennett A. Clements as he appeared during the Civil War. Courtesy of the National Library of Medicine, Bethesda, Maryland.

Indians; in all, over 2200 men. It was provided with rations for fourteen days, limited to hard bread, bacon, coffee, sugar and salt. Each officer and mounted man carried on his horse four days' rations, and one blanket for each officer and man was allowed. No tents or cooking utensils except tin cups were permitted, and no ambulances or wheeled

vehicles of any description taken. The rations were transported on two hundred and forty pack mules.

On the morning of August 5, 1876, the command left
its camp and wagon trains on Goose Creek, marching down
Tongue River, and on the 7th crossed westward to Rosebud
River, making a very hard march for the infantry of 22
miles, over a rough country and in blazing sun, and coming
upon a very large Indian trail which was followed down the
river until noon of the 10th instant, when a junction was
effected with the forces under Brigadier General Terry.
The united force continuing upon the trail, then turned to
the eastward and crossed Tongue river, and marching over
some "Bad Lands," encamped on Powder river on the
15th. Continuing down the Powder river, the Indian trail
was found to turn eastward at a point some ten miles from
its mouth; nevertheless the entire command proceeded to
the Yellowstone, at a point where the Powder empties into
it, arriving there on the 17th August, 1876.

Up to this time there had been but few men who
reported sick, though several heavy rainstorms had occurred. The command remained here, resting the animals
and waiting for supplies, until the morning of August 24,
1876. But few of our stock of medicines had been used, and
none of the surgical dressings; but I procured a few ounces
of quinine from General Terry's command and inasmuch as
it was supposed that we would of necessity reach some
point of supply at the expiration of the time for which we
were now freshly rationed—fourteen days—and as no estimation to the contrary was given, it was deemed unneces-
sary to make any further addition to the medical supplies.

On the 23rd of August, the day before leaving the
Yellowstone, thirty-four sick and disabled men were
transferred to the steamboat "Far West," of which number
fourteen were cases of acute dysentery and diarrhoea.

The night before our departure, a most violent storm

of rain and wind occurred, rendering sleep impossible, and saturating everything with water. On August 24th, at an early hour, the command moved out and marched up the Powder river. On the 25th General Terry arrived at our camp in advance of his troops, but returned the same evening, and thereafter General Crook's force operated alone. Leaving Powder river, the command now made long marches to the northeastward, finding but scanty grass and only alkaline and extremely muddy water, and on the 28th encountering a severe storm of rain and hail. . . .

For the three following days we either remained in camp or made very short marches, and the opportunity was embraced to construct some mule-litters (of which two had already been needed) and to organize their management. I was efficiently aided in this by the previous experience of Surgeon A. Hartsuff, U.S. Army, who was placed in charge of them; but fortunately there was need of only three to five of them for the next six days. It was also determined to keep the seriously sick (who were transported on the litters) in a spot when in camp designated as "the hospital;" but for this purpose there was but one tent fly, no bedding except four blankets, and no cooking utensils but the tin cups of the men, and one frying-pan borrowed from the packers. Nevertheless there was a great advantage in having all these men together.

I also at this time advised with the commanding general on the state of health of the command, and in regard to the necessity that would soon arise for antiscorbutics. Some experiments were here made, at the suggestion of the general, in the use of the cactus and the Indian turnip as food and antiscorbutics, but it was found impossible to procure or use them to any extent. At this time also, some of the medical officers reported a scorbutic tendency among the men, inferring its existence from the ascertained character of the diarrhoea then prevailing, and one case of probable scurvy was reported, but the patient never presented himself again, and the medical officer was afterwards satisfied that he could not verify his diagnosis. But one case occurred in the command (in the latter part of October) marked by stiffening of the ham tendons, and induration of the calf of the leg.

On August 31st we were on Beaver creek, a stream of pure and comparatively clean water, and remaining on it for several days, it was found on September 2d, that the cases of diarrhoea had decreased to about 2½ (two and a half) per cent of the command, for forty-nine cases in all, and thereafter the complaint continued to decrease, and soon after reaching the Little Missouri river, on September 4th, where an abundant supply of astringent berries was procured, it seemed to wholly cease, and the opposite condition prevailed.

The Indian trail which we had so long followed, was found to have entirely scattered at the Little Missouri, and the command continuing eastward, arrived on September 5th at Heart river, about one hundred miles west of Fort Lincoln, when the trail was abandoned, and the commanding general announced his intention to return to the south and reach the Black Hills. Long marches had been made in the midst of frequent rain-storms, with cold nights and heavy dews, and the prospect of achieving satisfactory results, always so encouraging to the soldier, was not apparent. There were but five and a half days rations of coffee, and less than two days of bread and salt left; the distance to the Black Hills was not definitely known, and the Ree Indian scouts, who alone knew anything of the intervening country, left us at this point to carry despatches to Fort Lincoln. Under these unfavorable conditions the command moved from its camp directly south on the morning of September 6th, and marched thirty miles over a broken, rolling country, and camped at some alkaline water holes, without enough wood to even boil coffee with. On the 7th we again made thirty miles over the same kind of country, and had an equally bad camp. All the litters, nine in number, were in use this day; many entreaties of sick and exhausted men had to be resisted; many horses were abandoned, and men continued to struggle into camp until 10 P.M. On this day the men began to kill abandoned horses for food. The sick and exhausted men of the infantry were carried on pack mules, whose loads were now used up, but only a small part of those applying could be so carried.

On the night of the 7th a command of 150 cavalry, with 50 pack mules, was sent forward under Captain [Anson] Mills, 3d Cavalry, with orders to proceed to the settlements in the Black Hills and return with food for our command.

On the 8th we marched twenty-four miles in a bitterly cold, driving rain-storm, and the ground being saturated with water, made progress difficult for both men and animals; but on reaching camp some wood was found, and it being thus possible to cook it, horse meat was issued to the command. It rained heavily all this night, but having fires, there was less discomfort than for the two previous nights.

On the 9th occurred the action of Slim Buttes. Soon after leaving camp a courier arrived from Captain Mills (who, as stated, had left us on the 7th to proceed to the settlements in the Black Hills) informing the general that he had discovered and attacked an Indian village. The best of the cavalry was immediately ordered forward, and being directed to send a suitable number of medical officers or go myself, I at once went in person, and ordered up the pack mules with medical supplies, and proceeded at a trot with the commander of the cavalry to the scene of the engagement, some fifteen miles in advance.

Arriving at the village (which was already in possession of Captain Mills's force) at 11 A.M. with the advance of the cavalry, and with the hospital pack mules immediately at hand, I at once proceeded to examine and dress the wounded, who had been collected in and about an Indian teepee, and was efficiently assisted by the medical officers of the cavalry as soon as they came up. Owing to a desperate resistance made by a few Indians concealed in a ravine from which they could not escape, a few wounded continued to be brought in, but by 3 P.M. all had been dressed and cared for, except one case of an officer requiring amputation, which was deferred until a consultation could be had. The teepee used as our hospital station was during this time repeatedly exposed to the shots of the Indians. At 4 P.M. a concerted attack was made on three sides of our camp (our entire force having meanwhile arrived) by the Indians who had been driven from the village in the morning reenforced by others from Crazy Horse's Band, in which a few more men were slightly wounded.

Before this attack began Surgeon [Albert] Hartsuff had been authorized to take some of the teepees for an hospital, but by some misunderstanding or lack of discipline, their selection for this purpose was not respected by our men when the village was given over to pillage, and he only succeeded by personal resistance and determined exertions in saving one of them. Into this some of the less severely wounded had been removed when the afternoon attack began, and it being exposed to the fire of the Indians, the nurses and wounded hastily left it, and before it could be again secured, it was torn down and carried away by our men. We were thus without any shelter for our sick and wounded except the tent-fly previously used. There was an abundant supply of surgical dressing, and the amputation was done, and all the wounds dressed by sundown; but we had no food for them except the dried meat found in the captured village, which it was difficult to eat, and impossible with our means to cook.

In this action one man was killed and fifteen wounded, including one officer, in addition to one citizen scout, killed. During the night additional litters were made at my request, and a company of cavalry detailed to escort and manage them under the immediate direction of Surgeon Hartsuff. A great number of fine lodge-poles suitable for litter-poles were found in the village, and I requested that some of them, with a large and fine teepee that Lt. Colonel Carr of the 5th cavalry had cheerfully placed at my disposal for the use of the wounded, should be carried along for future use; but notwithstanding it seemed almost certain that we would be attacked on the next march, the request was denied as being impracticable, though quantities of plunder, and much of it useless, was transported. Greater good fortune than, under the circumstances, it seemed reasonable to expect, attended us, however; and though our rear was attacked the following day, but one man was wounded.

On the 10th September, the day following the fight, we marched fifteen miles, having twelve litters in use, leaving three in the rear for emergencies. In the order of march the loaded litters were immediately in rear of the infantry, which always started in advance, while the unoccupied litters moved in front of the rear guard, where Surgeon Hartsuff remained to designate who should or should not be carried on them, a very harassing and sometimes responsible position. The cavalry who were sick, and those whose horses were abandoned or eaten, marched in rear of the litters, or as near to the infantry as possible.

On the 11th we marched twenty-one miles in a cold rain and bitter wind, the transportation of the wounded requiring extraordinary labor and care, on account of the "bad lands" through which we passed, and numerous ravines. The command had had no bread, bacon or salt since the 9th instant, and an order of August 30th, permitting hunting for the sick, under certain restrictions, had resulted in securing only two ducks and one leg of antelope—the latter contributed by a medical officer. Another leg of antelope was thus contributed, and the Acting Assistant Commissary having assiduously searched every bag or parcel in his charge, fortunately found some salt, half a pound of sugar, and two quarts of flour shaken from old sacks, upon which the sick and wounded made a meal, supplemented by a few cans of preserved fruit that had been scrupulously reserved for such an occasion, that cheered their spirits and gratified all that had the care of them.

The next day, September 12th, the command marched soon after daylight. Frequent showers of rain occurred during the day. At noon we suddenly came in sight of "Bear Butte," a prominent outlying spur of the Black Hills, and descending somewhat lower came upon a slightly rolling plain, which the rain had converted into a most tenacious quagmire. Men and animals struggled through it with difficulty; many of the latter were abandoned, and the saddles of abandoned or slaughtered horses, and even boxes of ammunition, "cached" to relieve the struggling pack mules. Some of the litter mules fell in crossing streams and ravines, or sank nearly to their knees in the tenacious soil, but none of their occupants received any injury. Thirty-four miles were made before the main body of the command reached camp on a tributary of the "Belle Fourche," at 9 P.M. The indomitable infantry column arrived at 10 P.M. —numbers of men were strewed exhausted on the line of march, and all did not arrive until noon of the next day. The litters with the wounded and sick reached camp at 9½ P.M.; it was difficult to pilot them in the inky darkness to the spot selected for them, and as soon as they were halted a great part of the men in charge left them, and neither the commands nor entreaties of the medical officers could induce them to return; exhausted by the harassing duties of the day, they disappeared in the darkness, to seek rest and sleep in a cold rain, without food and with scanty fire. Nevertheless, by the personal exertions of Surgeon Hartsuff and myself, aided by the Steward and a few of the more willing men, the mules were detached from the litters, and the latter being placed side by side with their occupants, a tent-fly and a teepee cover were spread over them, and some protection thus secured from the rain, which again fell heavily, and some hot coffee was soon after served out to them.

The following day we again moved out about 1 P.M., cheered by news that wagons with supplies were near at hand, and after marching five miles, and crossing our wounded and sick over the rapid "Belle Fourche" with difficulty, all the command encamped, with an abundance of wood and fine water. The sun suddenly shone out brightly, and before night wagons with supplies from the settlements in the Black Hills arrived; a double allowance of rations was issued and at last our perilous march was ended without death.

Forty days had passed since we left our supply camp on Goose creek. It had rained on 22 days, and for the previous nine days in succession, rain had fallen, often in great quantities, and for six successive days we had not seen the sun. No game of any consequence had been procured, and the diet of all, officers and men—sick and wounded alike—had at the best been scanty. Since leaving Heart river, on the morning of September 6th, we had marched 160 miles in incessant cold rains, with but little fuel, with bad water, without shelter, and almost without food, yet a report of sick on the day after our arrival at the Belle Fourche, showed that but 2.04 (two and four hundredths) per cent of the command were excused from duty by reason of sickness, and not a man had died except in battle or of wounds. Nevertheless, many men applied for treatment suffering from constipation, leg-weariness and debility. . . .

I have related at some length the circumstances of this march, to detail the existence of causes which ordinarily operate unfavorably to the health of troops, and to point more strongly to their apparent freedom from serious sickness. Yet it was manifest that they could not longer have borne these unusual privations, exposure and fatigue; they had reached the limit of human endurance, as an organized body, and it is unpleasant to contemplate the probable consequences of another march like that of September 12, 1876.

The impossibility of having wheeled vehicles, and the consequent want of ordinary transportation for the sick, imposes upon the medical officer the painful necessity of denying very many applications for transportation of men who were sick or exhausted. It is not to be doubted that had we been provided with these means, and had it not been known that there were no hospital tents or shelter for them, a very much larger proportion of men would have been reported sick. Hundreds of men remained "on duty" during the latter part of the march to the Belle Fourche, who, under ordinary circumstances, would have been excused and transported, and in recording the small proportion of sick on our arrival at this river, these circumstances must be considered, and should in justice be placed to the credit of the discipline and fortitude of our men. Nevertheless the duties of the medical officer was most exacting, demanding unwearied patience and exertion, and the use of every resource that ingenuity or experience could suggest. The service of the litters particularly required patience and fortitude on the part of the medical officers, both to appease the complaints and entreaties of stragglers and exhausted men, and to endure the spectacle of suffering it was impossible to relieve, and of the results of demoralization that they were powerless to prevent. . . .

The command moved from the Belle Fourche after a welcome rest of two days, to a new camp on Whitewood creek, five miles in advance, where, on the 16th of September, General Crook, transferring the immediate command to Col. Merritt, 5th Cavalry, left it, accompanied, among others, by one medical officer. The case of amputation, and that of gunshot fracture of the thigh, were moved on the

17th to Crook City, where every provision for their comfort that was possible was made, and were left in charge of Acting Asst. Surgeon C. R. Stephens, who was detached from the command for this purpose. Both did well, and remained at Crook City until November. The case of gunshot fracture was of the middle third of the thigh. I had applied, a few hours after the receipt of the injury, and after removing and detaching a number of fragments of bone, a plaster splint from the trochanters to the ankle, and he was transported 90 miles on a mule-litter over a broken country without experiencing any pain or notable disturbance. I venture to express my confident belief that by the use of plate splints and litters, many limbs, and many lives that otherwise would be sacrificed, will be saved in the future, even in civilized warfare. By making short marches, or laying over every few days, the needed rest was given to our men and animals, and I was enabled to provide more comfortably for our sick and wounded.

The strength of our department being reduced by two medical officers, I myself assumed charge of the hospital, and of the transportation of the sick and wounded, and having procured a teepee cover, an additional shelter was made. Authority was obtained from the commanding general, before his departure, for the purchase of such cooking utensils, clothing, &c., as might be necessary, and some articles of the former were thus procured on the 19th and on our arrival at Custer City on September 23d, all the utensils necessary, together with some underclothing and a few medicines, were purchased, and were of the very greatest benefit. . . .

We remained in the vicinity of Custer City, changing camp a few miles every few days, until October 17th and the larger portion of the cavalry, which had been detached on October 13th to scout to the north and eastward, having returned to the main camp on the 20th, the entire command then marched to Camp Robinson, Nebraska, near

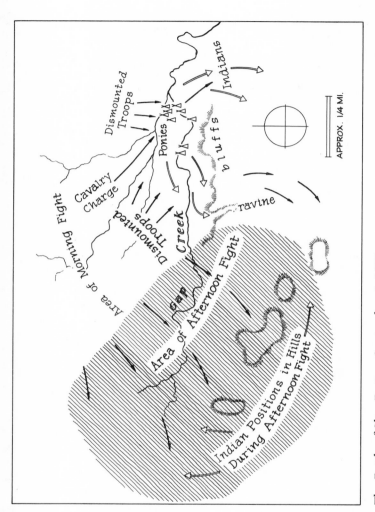

The Battle of Slim Buttes, September 9, 1876.

Red Cloud Agency, arriving there on the afternoon of October 24th. . . .

On January 24, 1914, Anson Mills detailed his recollections of the Battle of Slim Buttes to interviewer Walter M. Camp. Mills discussed his command's role in the morning assault on the village and in the fight with the Indians sheltered in the ravine. The manuscript reposes in the Camp Papers, Robert S. Ellison Collection, Papers, Diaries, Interviews and Comments, Item 7a, Denver Public Library.

[By September 7] Crook had got to some point in vicinity of the Cannonball [River] and horses were playing out fast. I, with my squadron, was rear guard & Crook ordered me to shoot all played-out horses & we shot 70 that day that we found turned loose as we came along. About ⅓ of the men were afoot, and some of the officers were afoot, especially those who had taken no extra horses along. I had two good horses. John F. Finerty was afoot and he did not like it because I would not permit him to ride my extra horse. There was nothing to eat . . . [and] we had been eating horse flesh.

When Crook made a bivouac that night he & [Colonel] Merritt were sitting together and on I came in with my squadron of 4 companies. Crook said he wanted me to pick 150 men out of the command & go to Deadwood for supplies. I was to get supplies and return and meet him, as he was to come on as well as he could with the rest of the command. I took 15 men from each of our 10 cos [companies] of 3rd Cavalry. Officers—[Lieutenant Emmet] Crawford, [Lieutenant Frederick] Schwatka, [Lieutenant Adolphus H.] Von Luettwitz and others. [Lieutenant John W.] Bubb had command of the 50-mule pack train that we had to bring back provisions.

We started soon after dark & marched all night slowly toward the west and until 2 P.M. next day. During the night we came up to a kind of lake or pond, where there was con-

Captain Anson Mills, Third U.S. Cavalry, whose troops attacked the Sioux village at Slim Buttes. Courtesy of the National Archives.

siderable water. [Scout Frank] Grouard struck a match & we saw the ground all cut up with fresh horse tracks & Grouard said there must be a large body of Inds near. Grouard kept a little way ahead—not far—and found the way as best he could. Grouard was ahead & made a sign & halt[ed] and came back & said he saw Inds ahead & that there must be a big village of them. I wanted him to go ahead & locate it & he made it evident that he did not want to. I said I would go with him. We went up ahead & saw part of their herd & a few tepees up among the trees. We heard dogs bark etc.

It had been raining all day & was cloudy. I went back & took council with my officers & the majority of them were in favor of attacking and so we decided to lie by and do it. We were then not more than 1½ or 2 miles from the village, so I ordered a countermarch and we went back and concealed the command in the deep depression (about 150 feet deep) through which the stream [we] were on flowed. There was a considerable current of water in this stream. It has been said that this was Rabbit Ear creek, but I am not certain about that. . . .

Crook had told me to pitch into anything I found on my route that I thought I could handle. I had not much confidence in Grouard as a fighting man, and so did not heed his fear that we would find a village too large for us. He had a splendid knowledge of the country, and knew the ways of the Indian, and was, undoubtedly the best guide we could have found for such knowledge as that, but in many ways he was not to be relied upon. I always regarded him as a coward and a big liar.

I gave orders to the officers not to permit any of the men to leave the ravine but we were wet and cold and I consented to permit them to build fires, which they did. After the fires had been built I saw a peculiar thing. The clouds were low and as they passed over us the light of the fires would illuminate them much as a search light does the sky on a dark night. I was afraid this would discover us to the Indians, but the weather was bad and they were not on guard.

We lay on the creek until about an hour before daylight, when I gave Schwatka 50 mounted men & started. We soon came up to a herd of ponies grazing & Grouard said, there are their horses, and I halted & told Grouard to go ahead & find the exact location of the village. Grouard went off and remained a long time, and when he returned I noticed that he had a new horse. He had been riding an Indian pony that was thin and nearly used up. He had gone up to the herd, unsaddled, caught a fresh horse out of the Indian herd & saddled it. He was acting so cowardly and hesitatingly, that I at once suspected he was getting himself in shape to get away should we get into a hot fight. I reproved him for staying away so long.

I was afraid the herd would smell us & stampede into the village, and scolded Grouard for having gone among them, but he was a good deal like an Indian and the ponies seemed not to take fright at him, as he was riding an Indian pony.

It was now fast coming light, and we could see a few of the lodges across a depression. They must (according to the best of my recollection) have been on the southeast side of the Slim Buttes, but there were no high buttes near the village.

I had told Schwatka to be ready to charge on the village the instant the pony herd would stampede, for I knew the minute they smelled us they would start and run into the village, and this is just what they did. I had the rest of the command dismounted except for the horseholders.

When the herd stampeded Schwatka followed them right into the village, riding through it and firing with pistols into the lodges. He chased the herd through it, knocking down and trampling over some of the lodges, and then turning the herd and came back with it to us. I had the dismounted men advance and begin firing on the lodges, which were laced up to keep up [out] the rain, but the Inds cut open the opposite sides and all of them got away except 17 who took refuge in a bend of the creek bed [actually a ravine adjoining the creek bed], which was dry except for rain water that had settled in it here and there. These Indians we could cover, or keep from getting away, and once in a while they would take a shot at us. Others got behind rocks and kept up a fire, so we did not crowd the village.

We were on a slope that faced the slope that the village was on, with a sort of coulee or depression between these two slopes, and to make my position secure I dug intrenchments on the top of the hill just back of where we were lying. The Inds which we had corraled in the creek had called out and said that there was a large body of Indians not far away and that they intended to hold out until assistance came. For this reason I dug intrenchments and determined to hold out there & send for Crook, who was some 25 or 30 miles back. While the fighting was going on Grouard cleared out and I did not see anything of him. He had very little physical courage on such occasions.

I now mounted three men, in succession, one after another, on fresh Indian ponies, and told each of them to ride back on the trail as fast as they could and tell Crook that I had a village & was trying to hold it and needed assistance. Von Leuttwitz had been severely wounded and we had no surgeon with us, so we needed Crook at all events.

Crook got there about 11 A.M. and came up to me & said, "Where is the village? I want to see it." I told him not to get too close, as some Inds were under cover and would fire on him. Nevertheless he started toward the village and no sooner did he expose himself than he was fired upon, a bullet passing very near to him. He then said he would drive the Inds out and ordered a charge on them. In this charge the scout [Jonathan] White was killed and some men wounded. There was a good deal of firing into the gully and finally Crook told Grouard to tell the Inds if they would come out their lives would be spared, but they seemed to be mistrustful. Finally two or three squaws made a break and came toward us. When the other Inds saw that we did not harm the squaws they all gave up and came out, one man ([Chief] American Horse) holding his bowels in his hand, his abdomen having been ripped open by a shot. They led him up to where a couple of our surgeons were standing. One of them looked at the wounded Indian and made no offer to do anything, but said "Tell him he will die before next morning." The interpreter told him this, but the Indian never flinched or betrayed any feeling.

After Crook came the men began to tear up the village, and in pulling over buffalo robes uncovered a little girl who had hidden herself. She broke loose and ran, but a soldier caught her and I had him bring her to me. She was a pretty child and began to cry, being terribly frightened. The men, who were very hungry, were eating wild plums and meat that we found in the village. Thinking that the child was hungry after hiding since morning, I gave her some plums and meat and she ate, and seemed to recover from the shock of her capture. I led her around with me and she seemed to go willingly. There had been a good deal of firing into the creek [ravine] where the Inds took refuge and when the men went in to carry out the dead I walked in to take a look, the little girl following me. Among the dead were two women badly shot up. As soon as the little girl saw these she began to cry, and all of a sudden, ran up to one of the bodies and fell upon it and threw her arms around it. The corpse was that of her mother, who was shot several times through the body. In clasping the dead body the face and arms and hands of the little girl had become smeared with her mother's blood, and the sight was enough to touch the heart of the strongest man. . . .

After Crook got there the Inds from a distance began to show up around on high ground & at one time they were reflecting mirrors down upon us from higher ground.

Chapter 9
The Spring Creek Encounters, October 11, 15, and 16, 1876
Oskaloosa M. Smith and Alfred C. Sharpe

Soon after Crook started for the Black Hills by way of Slim Buttes, Gibbon and Terry withdrew to their respective stations—Gibbon to Fort Shaw, Montana, and Terry to Fort Abraham Lincoln, Dakota. In accordance with directives from General Sheridan, Terry left Colonel Nelson A. Miles and the Fifth Infantry to winter at the mouth of Tongue River on the Yellowstone. Another contingent occupied a cantonment at Glendive Creek on the Yellowstone, downstream from Miles's Tongue River post. In the autumn, after the falling waters of the Yellowstone prevented supply steamers from ascending, troops of the Twenty-second Infantry at Glendive escorted wagon trains of provisions the 110 miles to Tongue River. On October 11, and again on October 15–16, the trains came under attack by Indians, precipitating several months of conflict for Miles and his command.

Contemporary accounts of the attacks on the Glendive–Tongue River wagon trains are rare. The two offered below afford detailed descriptions of the fighting during the so-called Spring Creek encounters. The author of the first is believed to be First Lieutenant Oskaloosa M. Smith, whose letter appeared in the New York Herald *on November 27, 1876. Smith was from Indiana and had served through the Civil War in his state's volunteer infantry. Commissioned in the regular army in 1867, he joined the Twenty-second Infantry two years later, serving on the Yellowstone expedition of 1873 and in the South, and remaining with the regiment into the 1880s, when he entered the Commissary Department. Smith retired from the army a major in 1900.*

Second Lieutenant Alfred C. Sharpe, who also wrote an account of the actions, had resigned from West Point in 1875 after sustaining a severe injury during cavalry drill exercises.

116

*Commissioned in the Tenth Cavalry in 1876, Sharpe transferred
to the Twenty-second Infantry in July and proceeded to his station at Glendive. He remained with the Twenty-second until
1893, often serving on detached duty as professor of military sci-
ence and inspector of national guard troops. During the Spanish-
American War, Sharpe served as adjutant general of the First
Division, Fifth Army Corps, and participated in the siege of San-
tiago, Cuba. In 1901 he was appointed major in the Adjutant
General Department.*

*Both Sharpe and Smith won brevets for "gallant service
in action against Indians" at Spring Creek in 1876. Their letters were reprinted in John S. Gray, "Sitting Bull Strikes the
Glendive Supply Trains,"* Westerners Brand Book *(Chicago) 28
(June 1971).*

*Lieutenant Smith wrote the following letter at Glendive
Cantonment on October 26, 1876. It appeared in the* New York
Herald *on November 27, 1876.*

DURING THE LAST CAMPAIGN OF THE SUMMER, commencing August 8 at the mouth of the Rosebud and ending at
this camp on the 6th of September, scarcely a wild Indian
was seen. The season of operations was ordered to close on
or before October 15th, and troops were ordered to be can-
toned for the winter at the mouth of Tongue River. The
entire 5th Infantry was sent there to commence building,
so that the troops and stores might be protected from the
severe winter climate, and no time was lost. Six companies
of 22nd Infantry were left at this point [cantonment at
Glendive Creek on the Yellowstone] to receive the stores
from the boats, which could go no further up the river, and
convoy them to Tongue River. Afterward, added to this
force were two companies of 17th Infantry. These were all
small companies, numbering about 35 men each. They had
performed the escort duty, making nearly three trips each
month with a train of 100 wagons, without molestations by
Indians, until the last trip.

On the 10th inst. at noon, the train left here, and that
night camped on Spring Creek, 14 miles out. The next

First Lieutenant Oskaloosa M. Smith, Twenty-second U.S. Infantry. Courtesy of the U.S. Army Military History Institute.

morning they were surrounded and attacked by a large number of Indians, and in the skirmish numbers of mules were wounded, which caused a stampede and some loss of animals. The escort was so harassed that they were compelled to either abandon several wagons and some property, or else to return to this place; the latter course they prudently pursued, arriving late on the evening of the 11th.

The train was refitted and started again on the 14th, the commanding officer of the station, Lt. Col. [Elwell S.] Otis, taking command of the escort, consisting of C and G of the 17th Inf., and G, H, and K of the 22nd Inf., being a force of 11 officers and 185 men. The roster of officers was as follows:

Lt. Col. Otis, 22nd Inf., Commanding

1st Lt. [Oskaloosa M.] Smith, 22nd Inf., Battalion Adjutant

Act. Asst. Surg. [Charles T.] Gibson, Surgeon

Co. C, 17th Inf., Capt. [Malcolm] McArthur, 2nd Lt. [James D.] Nickerson

Co. G, 17th Inf., Capt. [Louis H.] Sanger

Co. G, 22nd Inf., Capt. [Charles W.] Miner, 1st Lt. [Benjamin C.] Lockwood

Co. H, 22nd Inf., 1st Lt. [William] Conway, 2nd Lt. Sharpe

Co. K, 22nd Inf., Capt. [Mott] Hooton, 2nd Lt. [William H.] Kell

At 10 o'clock A.M. [October 14] the escort and train moved out gaily. The day was beautiful and every man was in good spirits, feeling that they would meet the enemy before returning. That night camp was made in the beautiful bottom of the Yellowstone, 11 miles away. Early in the evening a thieving pack of Indians approached the camp and were fired upon by the sentinels. They beat a hasty retreat, leaving a pony with all its trappings and a leg broken. There were no more alarms that night.

At daybreak the next morning [October 15] the train was on the move, drawn up in four lines and surrounded by the escort which was disposed as follows: advance guard, Co. H., 22nd; advance right and left flankers, Co. C, 17th; right flank rear, Co. G, 22nd; left flank rear, Co. G. 17th;

rear guard, Co. K, 22nd. It was Sunday morning and a prettier one never broke forth.

Upon gaining the entrance to Spring Creek three miles from camp, three men joined the train, who proved to be scouts from General [Colonel] Miles' command at Tongue River. They were en route, four in number, from General Miles with dispatches for Glendive Creek; on Saturday afternoon [October 14] they were attacked at Spring Creek by a large number of Indians, one of their number was killed, and all their horses were either killed or badly wounded. The remaining three men were driven into the bushes, were they kept the Indians at bay until the darkness of night let them escape and they were thus enabled to join our troops. The body of the dead scout was found and buried. He was not at all mutilated and his gloves were on; evidently the Indians had not found him, but his gun and ammunition could not be found.

About this time the Indians made their appearance on the left side and in front, and opened fire on Scout [Robert] Jackson and Sergeant [Patrick] Kelly, Co. F, 22nd Inf., who were mounted and in advance. They had run into a large party of Indians, and after discharging their rifles at them, they fell back, closely followed by about thirty, their clothing being literally riddled by bullets but their bodies entirely unharmed. These two men did a great deal of scouting, coming in close quarters several times with the Indians, and showed a great deal of pluck and bravery.

The number of Indians kept increasing; the left flank advanced and the advanced guard charged them, opening the way for the train, which was enabled to ascend to the high table land. Then to our front signal smokes were raised, which were immediately answered by some vast ones off toward the Yellowstone, and Indians were seen coming from all directions, until the train was surrounded by from 400 to 500. During this time we had gained the ridge and hills leading down into Clear Creek and here the

enemy had taken position expecting to prevent our progress, but skirmishers were sent ahead and the road was
cleared, so that we gained the creek and watered the stock
in full view of the foe. But they were not idle; they collected on the further side and set afire to the prairie,
expecting to burn us out and to advance under cover of the
smoke and signally defeat us, but our troops gallantly
charged them, answering the Indian yell, and drove them
in all directions, so that the train could move on, though it
had to pass rapidly over the line of burning grass.

As soon as the top land was reached beyond Clear
Creek, the enemy came in strong force against all parts of
the escort. There were eighty-six wagons to guard, but
they were in four lines and surrounded by our skirmishers.
The prairies were burning, the smoke was suffocating, and
the enemy hurled his whole force with desperation against
the train, bent upon its capture, so that he would be well
provided with food and ammunition, but they were kept at
some distance by the advance upon them of the skirmishers, and not a shot damaged the train. The roar of musketry
was terrific. There was no artillery; it was simply an infantry fight. They were repeatedly charged in front by C,
17th, and H, 22nd, and in the rear, which was the most
pressed, by G, 17th, and K, 22nd. Company G, 22nd, during all this time, had a galling flank fire upon them.

This was kept up under a march of 15 miles until
nearly 5 o'clock, P.M., when the train was corraled for the
night, and shots were still exchanged until 7 P.M., when it
became too dark to see. In this struggle a number of Indians were knocked from their horses; many of the latter
were killed and a number were running around riderless.
These Indians had never before come in close range of
infantry, or been subjected to such a musketry fire.

It was expected that they would the next morning be
on us again, but we moved quietly from our camp. After
going a mile or more a shot was occasionally fired. About

this time a note from Sitting Bull, written by a half-breed Frenchman [John Bruguier], was found on a stake near the road, demanding reasons for traveling over the road and scaring the buffaloes, and ordering the troops back, telling them to leave rations and powder or he would fight them again, and signed "your friend, Sitting Bull. Please write soon." No attention was paid to the letter.

After the troops had passed Bad Route Creek, seven miles from the night's camp, two men came forward bearing a flag of truce. They were allowed to enter the lines, and were found to be Indian scouts from Standing Rock Agency with dispatches from General [Lieutenant Colonel William P.] Carlin. They had been ordered to visit hostile camps on business and had just arrived that morning. They said that the hostiles had met with considerable losses the day before and wanted to come in to make peace. Word was sent to them that a few of their headmen might come in unarmed. They did so, stating that they were tired of fighting and wanted to make peace. They wanted ammunition to kill buffaloes, and food for present use, and they would leave at once. They were told that ammunition could not be furnished them, but a small quantity of rations would be given them, which was accordingly done and they left us in peace.

During this fight several men were struck with spent bullets, and only three men were wounded—Sergeant [Robert] Anderson and Private [John] Donohoe, Co. G, 22nd Inf., and Private [Francis] Wraggle [Marriaggi],Co. G, 17th Inf. The Indians were poor marksmen. Our men were under fire for a long time and it is wonderful that no more men were hurt. All of our troops showed great fortitude and bravery and many of the men were recruits. . . .

Lieutenant Sharpe wrote the following letter at Glendive Cantonment, October 28, 1876. It was published in the Chicago Tribune *on December 7, 1876.*

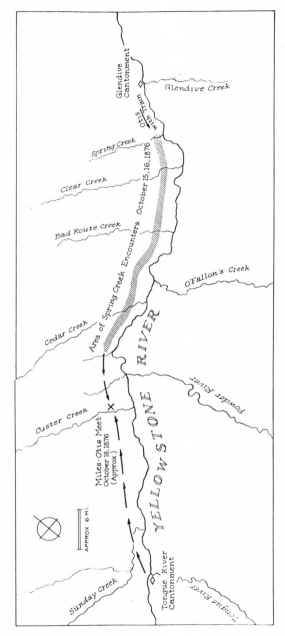

Glendive Cantonment

Glendive Creek

Spring Creek

Clear Creek

Bad Route Creek

Otis Train
with Train

October 15, 16, 1876

Area of Spring Creek Encounters

O'Fallon's Creek

Cedar Creek

YELLOWSTONE RIVER

Powder River

Custer Creek

Miles-Otis Meet
October 18, 1876
(Approx.)

APPROX 6 MI.

Sunday Creek

Tongue River
Cantonment

Tongue River

Area of the Spring Creek Encounters, October 11, 15–16, 1876.

. . . We left this place [Glendive Cantonment] on Tuesday, October 10th, with a valuable train of over one hundred wagons. The escort consisted of Co. K, 22nd Inf., Capt. Hooton and Lt. Kell; Co. C, 22nd Inf., Lt. Conway and myself. We encamped the first night on Deadwood Creek, about 14 miles from this post and about two miles from the Yellowstone. We had received intelligence, before starting, that 600 lodges of hostile Sioux had set out for the Yellowstone and that they probably intended to intercept us. All afternoon we noticed vast columns of smoke rising in the distant horizon; they were signal fires heralding our approach. At about 11 P.M. we heard the report of a musket, and upon inquiry, we ascertained that one of the pickets saw a man stealthily approaching our lines, who, upon being challenged, fled. Quiet was soon restored, and our camp was again wrapped in profound repose.

At 3:30 A.M. we were aroused by the sharp reports of a dozen rifles on the surrounding hills. Hurrying out of my tent, I saw the flashes of the muskets on the bluffs 500 yards distant. Bullets came hurtling and whistling by or tearing up the ground at my feet. Finally, their fusillade ceased—we did not return a shot. We busied ourselves getting breakfast and packing our tents and blankets for the march. Daylight revealed to us the loss of 57 mules. They had been stampeded and run off by the Indians.

At sunrise [October 11] we resumed our march. Scarcely had the rear guard—Capt. McArthur's company—got fairly under way, when they were attacked by a party concealed in a ravine 200 yards to our left, filled with underbrush and small trees. Capt. McArthur's company immediately deployed and charged the enemy, driving them over the bluffs and out of sight. Company H supported Captain McArthur's on the right. We then resumed our march, but had not advanced 80 rods, when they again opened fire—this time on the right flank. They were concealed in a ravine. A few shots were exchanged, but

Second Lieutenant Alfred C. Sharpe, Twenty-second U.S. Infantry, who was brevetted for his performance in the Spring Creek encounters. Sharpe is pictured as he appeared some years after the Sioux War. Courtesy of Jerome A. Greene.

without stopping the march. Looking back, we could see them literally swarming on our campground.

Their numbers were being rapidly augmented and they became bolder and more aggressive. All day long they hung on our rear, occasionally sending a ball whistling through our ranks. Embarrassed as we were by the loss of so many teams, the progress of our heavily-laden wagons was very tedious, and as the hostiles seemed to come swarming from every direction, now attacking us on the rear, on the flanks, and in front, it was decided to turn and fight our way through to Glendive. As we headed for home, the firing gradually ceased, the Indians seeming nonplused by this move. We arrived at this post about 9 P.M., Wednesday evening, October 11th.

After two days' rest, Col. Otis of my regiment took command, and increasing the escort to five companies by the addition of Company G, 17th Infantry, Major Sanger, we again set out [on October 14], determined to go through to Tongue River if fighting could take us there. We also had three Gatling guns. The first day we marched ten miles. That night at eight o'clock we were all "turned out" by a shot on the picket line. Two cavaliers had approached, and being challenged by the sentinel, turned in flight. But his swift bullet overtook them and next morning we discovered outside the line an Indian pony with a broken leg; it had saddle, bridle, blankets, and picket rope, just as they had been abandoned by the dusky rider the night before.

We resumed the march at about 7 o'clock [October 15]. It was the "peaceful Sabbath," a lovely day. My company was the advance guard, and as we strode along on that bright morning, I was thinking "how pleasant it would be to be away back in the States today to hear the church bells ringing and to see the good people coming into church;" and I almost imagined I could hear the sweet tones of the organ and the words, "The Lord is in his holy temple; let all the earth keep silence before him," when suddenly from

Lieutenant Colonel Elwell S. Otis, Twenty-second U.S. Infantry. Courtesy of the U.S. Army Military History Institute.

the bluffs ahead came the sharp, quick reports of musketry, and then the air was rent with screams and yells the most diabolical I ever heard. Two of our scouts had gone ahead and had discovered a large bank of redskins awaiting our approach. They sent a shower of bullets after the scouts, who came flying down the hill like mad men. The Indians were close upon them and, indeed, it was a chase for life. One of the scouts lost his hat. An Indian dismounted, picked it up, and rode off. One of the scouts had the cloth in the shoulder of his coat torn open by a bullet. The other had a hole through his moccasin.

My company was immediately deployed "left front into line" and I was detached with ten men from the right to take position on a very high hill on our right, while the main body of the company under Lt. Conway charged up the acclivity and after a short struggle, in which several Indian saddles were emptied, drove the enemy from the bluffs. The fight had now fairly opened and from that moment until the sun sank to rest—twelve long hours— we fought the fiends. About two o'clock, hot, thirsty, and weary, we reached Clear Creek—5 or 6 miles perhaps from our camp and about 16 miles from here. This creek flows through a deep, rocky ravine, two hundred feet below the level of the plain. The hostiles had taken a strong position on the opposite side commanding the valley and all approaches to the stream. But we must cross it, or consider ourselves defeated.

The Indians were hourly reinforced until now they numbered upwards of three hundred. We had but 180 muskets in line. One of the Gatling guns was placed in position, and under its cover my Company H, being the advance guard, made a rush for the valley; as we filed through it along the stream the Indians devoted their best shots to us. Sergeant H of my company was marching about two paces from me when he was struck with a thump in the breast by a spent ball, which fell, harmless, at his feet. They soon got the range and bullets came hissing about our heads and tearing up the ground all around and about us. Finally, we reached the foot of the opposite side, and with a cry, we charged up the hill. The Indians then set fire to the tall grass which was dry as tinder. The smoke was blinding and the heat intolerable, but rushing onward and upward, we gained the crest and again drove the villains before us. Panting and exhausted, the men sank down, completely overcome. But we had cleared the way, and we soon saw the long, white train of wagons climbing the hill.

The firing now became incessant. They were on all sides of us. We were completely surrounded. Down in the valley the reverberations of the musketry was deafening. As the train slowly climbed the hill and the rearguard— Company K, 22nd Infantry, Capt. Hooton and Lt. Kell— descended into the valley, the Indians closing in on them in great numbers. A report came that their ammunition was failing and another thousand rounds were sent back to them. Major Sanger then turned back to the relief of Capt. Hooton, as he was in imminent danger of being cut off. The enemy, having the vantage ground, waxed bold and charge after charge was made with varying success.

The prairie was fired all around us; we met the fires with counter-fires. Time and time again would they bring us to a dead halt, and a stubborn fight would ensue for possession of the road. Finally, the fire on the right flank ceased and they commenced enfillading our lines on the left, at the same time holding us at bay at front. Lt. Conway with ten men from the right of Company H was detached to go ahead and clear the way, while I was left with the remainder of the company on the left. Company G, 22nd Infantry, was advancing to our support; when about ten paces from us, I saw a man in its lines drop like a log; he was shot in the knee. After a half-hour halt, we again prevailed and wound onward. The prairie was ablaze all around us, rendering our passage in the road at certain places quite difficult.

The scene around me reminded me of the rhetorical descriptions we so often read of Napoleon's smoking wake. We left a blackened, desolate waste behind us. Perhaps our little conflict of a single day may not compare with his mighty struggles, but it was enough for about 180 men to attend to. Fighting a civilized enemy is perhaps rough work, but battling with fiends incarnate, highway robbers and midnight assassins, "shapes hot from Tartarus," together with fire, smoke, hunger and thirst, and the horrible fate of the captive at the stake in prospect is quite a different mode of warfare.

We were now on the high prairie, far enough from wood and water. The enemy had possession of the creek and to approach it was death. The sun was sinking below the horizon, and it was decided to form our corral and go into camp—if sleeping *a la belle etoile* can be called "camp." Rifle pits were dug around the entire corral at 500 yards from it, and you may believe there was little sleep in our camp that night. Every available man was on picket. I rolled myself up in a buffalo robe and with a canteen for a pillow slept with "one eye open." The firing had gradually subsided. The last shot was fired about 7 o'clock, and after making many attempts to burn us out by firing the prairie on every side, the fiends withdrew until the morrow. Their loss had been heavy. We saw many ponies running about riderless. One of our scouts came so close upon the Indians at one time as to kill one with a revolver. We had set out with 10,000 rounds of ammunition, 6,000 had already been expended, and here we were miles from the post and surrounded by the enemy. A gloomy prospect to be sure.

The next morning [October 16] they again opened on us just after breakfast. The fighting was not so heavy, but there was not a minute in the day that we did not have a bullet hissing by. I have always read of bullets whizzing and hurtling. They could not have come from Indian muskets. Their bullets hiss. The firing gradually subsided by 11 A.M., and the Indians began assembling in a body on an eminence half a mile ahead of us. One of their number had a white flag and wore a white jacket. As we approached he came at a gallop, accompanied by another with a white handkerchief, or rag, on his head. They presented Col. Otis a letter from Col. Carlin, commanding at Standing Rock [Agency, Dakota], certifying that they were friendly scouts, had just arrived from Standing Rock, and were en route to hostile camps on official business. They also presented the Colonel a letter from Sitting Bull, which you have doubtless already seen in the official reports. They said Sitting Bull was encamped nearby and desired to have a pow-wow.

Half an hour later a glittering cavalcade approached and was received by the Colonel. Sitting Bull [Sharpe misidentified this Indian] declined to dismount, and had a private secretary whom our interpreter had to address, and who then communicated with General Sitting Bull. After half an hour's talk, in which they were "mad" because we were running through their country and driving all their buffalo away, it was agreed that Uncle Sam should give four boxes of crackers and three sides of bacon, in consideration of which *res frumentaria* they would no longer molest us. The food was left in the road and we moved on. As a method of expressing his profound gratitude, one warrior brought up his gun and sent a bullet hissing over our heads, just to frighten us perhaps—the cunning creature.

The rest of our march was not at all exciting, except when the buffalo began to increase in numbers. We saw thousands of them, also of antelope. There is abundance of game in this country and the climate is simply glorious. It is all a delightful experience to me, of course. . . .

Chapter 10
The Battle of Cedar Creek, October 21, 1876

James W. Pope

The following selection continues coverage of the events of October 1876 after Colonel Otis's encounters with the Sioux. The ensuing days were significant in the course of the war for two reasons. First, Colonel Miles's meetings with Sitting Bull on October 20 and 21 became the first face-to-face confrontations by a federal official with a representative leader of the Indian coalition. Second, the battle of October 21 impressed the Sioux with the fact that Miles fully intended to press them forcefully and carry the fight to its inevitable conclusion. Cedar Creek thus constituted the beginning of an innovative policy by Miles that he would pursue for the duration of the conflict with the Sioux and Cheyennes.

The chronicler of this selection is believed to be Second Lieutenant James W. Pope, Fifth Infantry, who signed his article as "P." His description of the events at Cedar Creek was published in the Army and Navy Journal, *a tabloid for military personnel, on February 10, 1877. Pope's identity as author was easily deduced. He was the only officer in the regiment whose name started with P; moreover, he prominently discussed the work of his unit, Company E, in the fighting and was known to have reported campaign events for eastern papers. Pope was born in Louisville, Kentucky, in 1846 and graduated from the U.S. Military Academy in 1868. He spent that part of his army career in the West participating in Miles's campaigns on the Southern Plains and in Montana during the 1870s. During the 1880s Pope won promotion to captain and commanded the military prison at Fort Leavenworth, Kansas. In the Spanish-American War he served as a lieutenant colonel and chief quartermaster for volunteer troops in the Philippines. Pope retired in 1910 as chief quartermaster of the Department of Colorado. He died in Denver in 1919.*

Second Lieutenant James Worden Pope, Fifth U.S. Infantry, as a West Point cadet, 1868. Courtesy of the Special Collections Division, U.S. Military Academy Library.

. . . THE CUSTER DISASTER HAS IMPRESSED ALL MINDS
with a rather exaggerated idea of the number, power, and
daring of the Sioux Indians. This feeling, added to the
delay beyond the expected time of the supply train [from
Glendive], and the fact that Indians had been seen along
the way, caused an intense anxiety for its safety to be felt at
the Tongue River Cantonment. Gen. [Colonel] Miles, having sent scouts out to ascertain the cause of delay and
having received their report that they had seen nothing of
it, ordered the 5th Infantry to move across the river at once
with fourteen days' supplies, leaving the two companies of
the 22d to guard the cantonment. Everything was soon
across, and at 11 o'clock A.M. on the 17th of October, the
long column of the ten companies of the 5th, collected
together for the first time since the Utah ["Mormon"] War,
[1857–58] stretched out its serpentine length along through
the ravines leading northward from the Yellowstone. A
rapid march of twenty-eight miles that day and night, and
eleven the next morning, carried the command well up on
Custer Creek, where a small party of scouts were observed
in front, who speedily came up and reported that four of
them had fought twelve Sioux, one of their number having
been killed; and that the train was in sight. The train soon
followed . . . and the two commands encamped. The next
morning each pursued its way, the train on to Tongue
River and the 5th Infantry to punish those Sioux who had
so boldly struck a blow at its supply train.

The command moved along the Glendive road, seeing
no indications of Indians until the afternoon of the 20th,
when two were seen coming over a hill bearing a white
flag. These were the same Indians who had been to Col.
Otis, and they stated that Sitting Bull wished a council with
the commander. Too many important military considera-
tions—such as ascertaining the whereabouts, numbers,
arms of the band, and the character of their hitherto mythi-
cal leader, Sitting Bull, etc.—were involved in granting

this interview, in addition to the human desire to receive the surrender of such as decided to yield, to cause the request to be refused. Gen. Miles decided at once to grant the council and so notified the flag bearers. Between two and three hundred Indians soon appeared over a ridge some six hundred yards distant, and drew up in a line. Some difficulty was experienced in arranging the preliminaries, owing to the suspiciousness of the Sioux, and the absence of an interpreter, but Lieut. [Hobart K.] Baily [Bailey], Acting Adjutant, went over to the hostiles with the flag bearers, and found with Sitting Bull, a half breed [John Bruguier] who spoke English perfectly. All was, after some delay, settled, and Gen. Miles with his staff and orderlies rode out to the centre and twelve chiefs, dismounted, walked out in line to meet him. The command was drawn up in line on a ridge parallel to that of the Sioux, a Rodman gun with a supporting company on one flank, and a company on a hill on the other. A long consultation was then held, some of the chiefs being inclined to yield, but Sitting Bull obstinately demanding the cessation of the passing of trains and the withdrawal of the troops along the Yellowstone. The Indians were observed to be armed with Henry, Sharps, and Spencer rifles, many with carbines, tolerably well mounted, and poorly clad.

Sitting Bull appeared a stern, unyielding savage, with an intelligent, rather brutal face, and a powerful frame. He was evidently the war chief, speaking but little though bearing great authority. The Indians gathered thickly around the council circle, coming and going frequently during the colloquy. Nothing was effected, however, and the council quietly dissolved with the understanding that it should be renewed the next day. This was done more with the idea of preventing the Sioux disappearing than of gaining their surrender. The Indians quickly withdrew and the command moved back to Cedar Creek, some eight miles distant, where it camped for the night. This backward movement was made from the knowledge Gen. Miles had gained of its being the nearest water attainable in the direction of the Indian camp, and to encourage their hope of his withdrawing.

Early next morning, Oct. 21, the command took up the march northward, whither the Indians had gone the previous day, and had only proceeded a few miles when Indians showed themselves on a high knoll in front. Line of battle was rapidly formed in front, a skirmish line on each side of the train, in which order the advance was continued until the knoll was reached on which the Sioux had appeared. The white flag having again been displayed, the line was halted along a commanding ridge—a company sent to take possession of a second high knoll in front of the first. Here Indians and soldiers freely mingled, the former having become reassured by the previous council. Sitting Bull still retained his suspicions and made difficulties, especially fearing the Rodman gun planted on the knoll first mentioned.

The interview was finally arranged to take place on a little rocky butte in front of both forces, and this time an equality of force was enforced by sending one by one soldiers from the command, as Indians would ride up to the circle. On reaching the ridge on which the line was halted, the main force of the Sioux was beheld for the first time, those at the previous council being but a small part. In numbers, they certainly appeared formidable, for all the hills and valleys beyond, even into the dim blue ridges on the horizon limits, extended the swarming array of warriors. A dark mass beyond the range of distinctive vision clouded a high rise far in front, and indicated a still greater reserve. Some six hundred warriors only were absolutely determinable. . . . One thousand lodges have since been learned to have been at the time under Sitting Bull and his chiefs.

The council lasted until the afternoon, many of the

more tractable chiefs being decidedly disposed to yield, one actually offering himself as hostage for his band. This indication of yielding angered the stern old chief, and it has since been reported that he said then he was going to kill Gen. Miles, and attempted to carry out the threat, but was prevented by the more tractable chiefs. However this may be, he finally broke off from the council in anger, which caused the whole to hurriedly dissolve, the Indians hastily riding off and the whites quietly moving back to the command.

On the dissolution and failure of the council, the main body of the Sioux rode rapidly forward and took position on a commanding rise a few miles in our front, but many lingered on the nearer knolls and ridges as though waiting to see what next would be done. These were soon gratified. Gen. Miles had given a parting message to Sitting Bull repeating his demand that he yield himself and followers to the orders of Government, to send his reply quickly or he would open with his guns. As soon as the General reached the front of his regiment, the long wished for command "forward" was given and responded to with the utmost alacrity. The field for the fight, now evidently before the command, was one of great difficulty to an attacking force, a series of high ridges, commanding eminences, intersected by difficult ravines. The deep ravine of Cedar Creek extending along the right, if followed up, turns across the front thence treading to the front again, sending forward an off shoot perpendicular to the right, also bending around across the front. The main body of the Sioux were on the high rise beyond this creek and between ravines. On the further left was a very high ridge commanding the whole field; on the further front, a succession of rises gradually increasing in height. On front, right, and left also rose high gravelly knolls. The plan of Sitting Bull is disclosed by the nature of the ground so admirably adapted to Indian manoeuvring. This was to yield in front, and then while the

troops pressed forward and became entangled in the ravines to pour his warriors around the flanks and rear, and
play his magazine guns upon the disordered mass.

The command after moving forward in line a few hundred yards opened out in beautiful order into skirmishers,
and a company on each flank was detached to the right and
left to clear ridges and knolls still crowned by Indians.
There were but few on the left, which hastily gave way
before Co. A (Major [Captain James S.] Casey's), but some
fifty or sixty had collected on a knoll on the right up which
Co. K (Capt. [Lieutenant Mason] Carter's), moved stur-
dily, and though the Indians stood until the company was
quite close, they finally took to flight. The Sioux were now
fairly outflanked by the long wavy line of skirmishers, and
compelled to take positions directly in front, a state of affairs fatal to Indian manoeuvring. In this order, the line
entered and passed through the first ravine and up the hill
towards the main body of the Indians, Co. K (Capt. Carter)
on the right; Co. I (Major [Captain Wyllys] Lyman), Co. C
(Capt. [Edmond] Butler), Co. B (Capt. [Andrew S.] Bennett), and Co. A (Major Casey), in the main line; Co. H
(Lieut. [David Q.] Rousseau), Co. G (Lieut. [Theodore F.]
Forbes), and Co. E (Lieut. [James W.] Pope) in reserve;
Co. F (Capt. [Simon] Snyder), supporting Rodman gun,
and Co. D (Lieut. [Robert] McDonald), rear guard of the
train. There had not yet been a shot fired, Gen. Miles
desiring not to be first to break the late armistice, though
the advance fairly ended it. Once already the Rodman had
been unlimbered and sighted on the main body of Sioux,
crowded on a hill a mile from it, still we magnanimously
forbore.

As the long, undulating line of skirmishers moved up
the hill as before described, the Sioux commenced their
first hostile demonstration by riding in rapid circles, hang-
ing over the sides of their ponies. They could not stand the
steady, fearless advance, and retired sullenly before it. Still

there was no firing. Some Indians were observed firing the prairie; an order to stop which caused the first firing. As the Sioux retired from the front a number of them speedily took to the ravines and again endeavored to gain the flanks and rear in which a few were successful, while a greater number took possession of the lofty ridge on the left. Scarcely had the first shot echoed from the hills and ravines ere a rapid firing began in front and left rear. The latter, Co. E, was ordered to clear while Co. H (Lieut. Rousseau), was directed to take the lofty hill on the left. The latter movement was beautifully performed, the little company looking like a slender thread as it fearlessly pressed up the almost perpendicular height—while the Indians poured a rapid but harmless fire over their heads, and the key to the field was soon won.

Meanwhile the main line continued to advance, now pouring a rattling fire on the Sioux who, from behind hills, returned it, or dashing forward in wild circles and delivering a rapid fire from Henry rifles, would fleetly seek cover followed by the showers of bullets that responded. To add to this exciting scene, the fire started by the Sioux soon enveloped the whole front and added its fire and flame through which the tide of battle flowed. The rapid fire of the breech-loaders rolled like thunder. Cos. I and K passed through the Indian camp where were stored tons of dried meat and quantities of camp utensils. Here the Indians made their best stand, but could not stop the now victorious march of the troops, and gave way from the entire front, pursued for several miles. On this part of the field one private [John Geyer] of Co. I was severely but not fatally wounded.

Meanwhile, Co. E, having cleared the rear ravines, was left back to guard the train, while crossing the second ravine, and the Sioux now gathering on the flanks and rear again as the line moved forward, kept up a sharp shooting fire on this company from behind knolls and ridges. Here

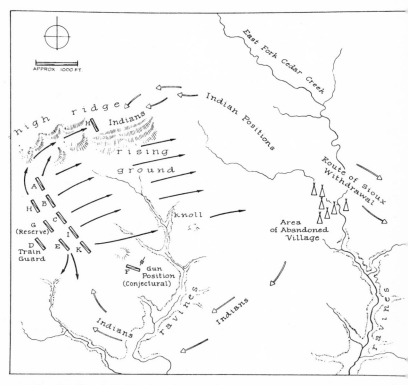

The Battle of Cedar Creek, October 21, 1876.

Sergeant [Robert W.] McPhelan, of this company, was severely wounded. The Sioux were now routed on all sides, and had entirely disappeared except a few in rear, where were the water holes necessary for the command. Co. E was now directed to clear out these and hold them for the night, while the command moved back and encamped on the high ridge taken by Lieut. Rousseau. It is impossible to determine the loss of the Sioux in this engagement, for the reason they fought from behind hills chiefly, and could carry off their dead, which they invariably do. Six dead

bodies were reported seen on the field. Their principal loss
consisted in the large quantity of dried meat, camp equip-
age and utensils found in their camp.

The next morning, a party of about twenty Sioux made
a dash at a straggler, but were driven off by a rapid fire
from Co. E. The command soon after moved out in skirmish order eastward, soon striking a very extensive lodge
pole 'trail, and pressed rapidly forward on this, Sioux [war-
riors] constantly seen at a good distance on flanks and in
rear. These continually lighted the prairie to the windward, and through the blackened and burning waste the
command pressed onward, stimulated by these evident
manoeuvres of the Indians to delay the march, and hopeful
that the Yellowstone, towards which the trail was bending,
could not be crossed before the command should catch the
fugitives. All along the line of march were strewn in increasing quantities abandoned and dead ponies, lodge
poles and other property lost in a hasty fight. Among these
appeared articles bearing "7th Cavalry," marks showing
that these same Sioux were part of those who slaughtered
the gallant Custer and his brave soldiers.

Toward evening a norther came up and the fire lighted
by the Sioux came raging through, and sweeping down the
tall dry grass so swiftly that a halt became necessary to burn
the prairie in front, when the whole command was enveloped in the seething smoke, fiery flames and blackened
ruin, the men looking like spectres in the weird, shimmer-
ing heat. . . . [During this episode] some Sioux made a
charge on a few scouts, [and were] replied to by a fire from
Co. K, which fight occurring in the wild, weird scene
formed a grand spectacle of savage warfare. The next day
not an Indian was to be seen as the command hastened on.
The order of march was now changed to one which will
commend itself to a military mind. A grand hollow square
of skirmishers was formed, four companies on the front
line, two on the sides, two in reserve held opposite the rear

of the square so that by forming line to the right and left and deploying, the sides are extended; one company in rear of the train which is partly within the square, one with the Rodman gun. Such a line like vertebra can be bent in any direction without disorder and without any change of order, and cannot be broken by an irregular cavalry. Such a formation presented a magnificent and formidable picture as it swept over the prairies. The pursuit of the retreating Sioux was vigorously pressed to the Yellowstone, only to find they had crossed a little before the command reached it. The next day, a party of a dozen Indians were seen at their place of crossing and were pursued to the hills by a party of scouts where a skirmish took place. The Indians retreated, but whirled round and made a furious dash at a herder who had gone out to kill some stray ponies. It was an exciting scene, the man urging his mule for dear life, chased by a dozen Indians, scouts charging to save him and infantry also madly rushing for the same purpose. Just then the Rodman thundered forth, the shell lighting just in front of the Sioux, who turned about and dashed as wildly for the hills as they had toward the herder.

The above related skirmish occurred Oct. 24th, and was the last affair with these Indians, and thus in seven days the command had broken the prestige of Sitting Bull, had beaten the formidable body of warriors he had collected to prey upon the line of supply, had cut it into fragments and pursued the main body across the Yellowstone, deprived the whole of a large part of the winter supply and a quantity of much needed robes, utensils, etc. To render all these losses irreparable it was necessary to continue the pursuit. The remaining rations were, however, wholly inadequate for the purpose, and must be replenished. The command had now reached a point only twenty-four miles from Glendive, one depot of supply. Indians were still seen hovering around the camp on the opposite side of the river. These were evidently watching with intense anxiety to see whether the command would cross. A proposition was made to these that a council be held the next day, to which they eagerly consented. That night the train started in to Glendive for supplies. The council was held, these Sioux being greatly subdued by the preceding events, although their demands were still such as could not be entertained; willing to promise anything but unwilling to give pledges. The council broke up unsatisfactorily, the Indians agreeing to return the next day.

The supply train returned early the next morning with twenty days' supplies and everything was in readiness for a renewal of the pursuit. The Sioux chiefs returned and the council again opened. Red Skirt (prominent in the Red Cloud council a few years ago), Ball Eagle [Bull Eagle] and Small Bear were the representative chiefs, and had been eminent in the Sitting Bull council circle. Red Skirt opened by a long speech saying that his Indians were going into the agency, that they were poorly clad, ponies worn down, hungry, that they did not want to fight any more but wanted to hunt buffalo, wanted the troops not to cross the Yellowstone, not to follow his people, that his young men would not like it, wanted the troops to return to the Tongue River post. In fact his wants were quite numerous. The others followed in the same strain, the apparent burden of the whole being that they were in a very bad condition and, unable to endure further pursuit, earnestly desired peace. They were told in reply that such talk would not do and must cease; it was endeavored to be impressed upon them that such would do for victor but scarcely for vanquished; it was conveyed to them that U.S. troops were in the habit of going whithersoever the Government ordered, however sadly it might interfere with the inclination of their young men; it was explained to them that if they desired peace it could only be obtained by complying with the orders of the Government. They were finally told that abundant supplies for pursuit had just arrived, and in case they refused such terms as were offered, they would be immediately followed.

All this was kindly but emphatically explained to them, and the effect was instantaneous. Their talk altered at once, and showed they were only endeavoring to get the best terms possible, having made up their minds to surrender. These terms were quite liberal, viz., that they go into their agency and there submit to the orders of the Government; that they deliver up to be sent around by Fort Buford and St. Paul five of their chiefs or head men as hostages, and as they were quite destitute sufficient rations were to be furnished them to take them in. These terms were speedily agreed to; Red Skirt himself being one of the hostages, and Bull Eagle and Small Bear promising to take the tribes in. In this surrender were included over six hundred lodges, comprising all the hostile Minneconjous and Sans Arcs except Gall's (or Yellowliver's) band of twenty lodges. These Sioux were bitter against Sitting Bull, seemed desirous of having him captured, told that he had broken off with his own (about fifty) lodges and gone North. The next day, Oct. 27th, the chiefs were surrendered, the rations given, the former sent under guard to Gen. Terry at St. Paul, where [whence] the two parties separated, the Indians for their agency and the 5th Infantry for new operations against Sitting Bull.

Chapter 11

The Fort Peck Expedition, November 6– December 13, 1876

"Regular"

Colonel Miles returned briefly to the Tongue River Cantonment after the Cedar Creek battle. On November 6 he launched the Fort Peck expedition, which took the Fifth Infantry north into the largely unknown wilderness between the Yellowstone and Missouri drainages. For more than a month columns from Miles's command tramped through the region after Sitting Bull and his warriors. The march was impeded by subzero temperatures, snow squalls, and difficulty in fording a Missouri River filled with treacherously cascading ice floes.

Details of the expedition are here recounted by an unidentified man of the Fifth Infantry. The account was published in the Leavenworth Daily Times *on February 18, 1877.*

WITH A CONFIDENCE GREATLY HEIGHTENED by the past remarkable campaign, the 5th Infantry turned faces to the northward with a wagon train, bearing thirty days supplies, the direction being towards the Big Dry river and Fort Peck on the Missouri. . . . Soon reaching Sunday creek, a most difficult country presented itself, broken by an infinitude of deep ravines, requiring constant digging and bridging, to get the heavily loaded wagons along. Leaving this and striking over the high, rolling divide, where immense herds of buffalo and antelope literally lined the flanks of the command, the latter running alongside often for miles, a long day's march brought the 5th to an eastern tributary of the Big Dry. Thence again over the high divide to the main stream, and down the broad, sandy bottom, immense sand dreins [drains] occasionally appearing along the sides. The first signs of Indians were seen in recently killed buffalo, and a small lodge pole trail. Heretofore, the morning start had been before daylight, and, under a bright norther moon, and a heaven studded with brilliant stars, progress had been easy, but now came a blinding, thin, misty, snow storm, driven by a keen norther, rising to a cold snow, bringing the mercury down to ten degrees below zero. Not even this detained the command more than one day, during which Co. E and Co. H were searching the trail lost by the snow.

The trails were found treading towards Fort Peck, and on down the bottom of that now frozen river, with wagons breaking through, mules tumbling in, but by herculean exertions the troops overcame all, marching twenty-three miles—still moving down the thousand-yard-wide bed of that well-named stream. A large Indian camp was reported ahead by the scouts and mounted men could be plainly seen going over a hill far in advance. Under the first exhilarating excitement of the march, the troops eagerly pushed forward when suddenly at the foot of the lofty bluff the "King of Rivers" burst upon our view at Fort Peck. It was the great Missouri no longer dark and muddy, but clear as crystal, rolling rapidly under a surface frozen over completely. The burst of excitement that ran through the ranks, and frequent reference to [Fort] Leavenworth [where the Fifth had recently been stationed] told how vividly the sight of the familiar old river carried back their memories. This river is the same even this far up in its general characteristics, its shifting channel, its raging current, its bank-teeming propensity, but its water is quite clear and its width a few hundred yards. Fort Peck is the agency of the Yanktonais, Assiniboins and Gros Ventre Indians and has long borne the evil reputation of being the base of supplies of ammunition and centre of operations of the hostile Indians, especially Sitting Bull.

Additional and gratifying results of the [recent] victory

over Sitting Bull and the present move were soon learned. No less than thirteen chiefs and one hundred and nineteen lodges of those lately encountered in the field were found to have been driven in by this movement or to have come in shortly after the battle of Cedar Creek. Among these were Iron Dog, a chief said to be of co-equal authority with Sitting Bull, a son of Black Moon, called a greater [chief] than the latter, and others of almost equal importance. Very interesting accounts of the fight were learned here from the friendly Indians and the half-breed interpreter of Sitting Bull, also found here. These accounts say there were 1,000 lodges in the fight, that the Indians fought as well as they could, but had never seen so many men on foot or that shot so well; that Sitting Bull had entirely lost his prestige and influence with the other chiefs, and had only his own fifty or seventy lodges with him.

Although the troops were highly pleased at these satisfactory results of their operations, the status of affairs at that agency was calculated to engender feelings of quite a different nature. From a rather free intercourse at the second council, the soldiers became acquainted with the faces of many of the hostiles, and here again met them strolling freely and leisurely about this government agency with Henry rifles; saw one present his ration ticket and get his seven rations, a state of affairs such as was never before recorded in the history of government. While these government troops were out enduring all the rigor of this frigid clime, while making long, toilsome, difficult marches, here were the Indians, for the punishment of whom all this endurance and labor were undergone, comfortably sheltered and protected, some fed and clad by a branch of the government. We want, partially at least, fair play. We don't mind fighting against odds, but in the matter of endurance of this climate the Indians, having had a life-long training, and thereby having a great advantage, should be kept out while troops are out. There is nothing to prevent those Indians driven into Fort Peck from going out into [the] field in the spring, recruited in numbers, reinvigorated by repose in winter quarters, with ponies fattened and supplies renewed.

Further information received here, showed that there remained now in the field the Cheyennes, somewhere on the Big Horn river; Crazy Horse's band, further south, and the band immediately with Sitting Bull, reported near Pine Butte, west of the Big Dry. This point was approachable from two directions, one north of the Missouri, and the other south, and accordingly the command was divided, companies "A," "B," "E," "G," "H" and "I" moved across the frozen Missouri, causing fearful trepidation among the "friendly" Indians, and refreshed by a few days' rest, drew out November 19th and made long strides toward the west, accelerated by the information that Sitting Bull was going to corral a little trading settlement on the Missouri to procure ammunition.

Soon entering a country more difficult than any before encountered, a few days struggling with ravines and slipping, frozen and snowy ground, bridge building and road making all along the way, brought the command into the beautiful, wood valley of Frenchman's creek, where the eye could not gaze anywhere without encountering buffalo and antelope, in the rounded knolls along the undulating ridges, over the long rises, in the deep waving grass, every where the herds of antelope large and small would gather and flee and scatter and wind round and the enormous herds of buffalo take the undulating gallop to and over the hills; elk, white and black tail deer, prairie chickens, sage hens, all such game is so plenteous as would make Frenchman's creek truly a paradise for a hunter.

Proceeding down this valley at first with not a single tree but soon well timbered, the 25th brought us to a road leading to Carroll where Capt. [Andrew S.] Bennett's company, reinforced somewhat, was detached to ascertain the correctness of the report of the sale of ammunition, and to seize any such as was for that purpose. The command moved on down the valley west, and entering Frenchman's creek, and a few miles brought the grand old Missouri once more in view, with its wide heavily timbered valley, a sight to delight the souls of the frosted, benumbed soldiery. Under the tall cottonwood trees and in the thick under- brush, herds of deer and elk were seen reposing; so nu- merous were these that two small parties permitted to hunt, in a few hours brought in a couple of deer and eight elk. However pleasant the delightful valley and tall trees and tangled underbrush, such as could defy the coldest, fiercest norther, might be, one difficulty at once presented itself tending to detract therefrom—the question of cross- ing—for the river was now broken up, and the great blocks and floes of ice were hurrying down its swift narrow chan- nel. Its presence must be undertaken, however, and on the day of arrival, men were set to work to build a large raft, and until far into the night might be seen the weird picture of a huge fire in a deep entangled forest, figures hammer- ing, carrying, moving about in the dark shades, ac- companied by the merry jest, loud laughter and lively chat- ter of the crowd of busy men.

Early on the morning of [the] 26th, the raft, which had been constructed with so much labor the evening before, was, by great exertion, launched into the rapid torrent and towed up a couple of hundred yards above the mouth of Squaw Creek, where it was desired to effect a landing. Here General [Colonel] Miles accompanied by Lieuten- ants [Frank D.] Baldwin and [James W.] Pope got on board with a crew of twelve men armed with long cotton wood poles and pushed out on the perilous voyage. As soon as the raft left the shore the difficulty of the passage fully appeared, the depth of the river being so great that the twenty feet [foot-long] poles little more than struck bottom and the current almost carried overboard those endeavoring to use them. Rapidly born down the swift stream making but little progress, the raft passed Squaw Creek before half the passage was effected, and below frail ice extended out towards the centre of the river. Still the men worked vigorously, when suddenly the raft was carried with immense force full upon a huge snag and with a fearful jar stuck fast, the men being nearly thrown off by the shock, causing great confusion. To add to the horrors of the situation, a rapid firing was heard, and the cry that the pickets were firing, arose. A more desperate situation could scarcely be conceived. Imprisoned on a frail raft in the middle of the most dangerous of rivers with a crowd of unarmed men close by, huddled together, and the prospect of an attack from the opposite shore staring them in the face, huge blocks of ice rushing down upon the craft, all combined to form a situation of utter apparent helplessness. However, the clear voice of the General rang out above the clamor, ordering the assembly sounded, the banks lined, the cause of the firing ascertained, a boat (which had been constructed of a wagon bed covered with canvas) sent out.

The firing was ascertained to have been done by hunters and the attempt to get a rope across was resumed. The canvas covered wagon bed succeeded in reaching the raft, the men using spades for paddles. The rope which was to be stretched across the river was on the raft and the central position was of advantage as one point of fastening. The wagon bed was now sent over to the opposite shore with the rope, and this was secured to the opposite shore by Private [Thomas] Kelly of Company "I," boldly venturing over the frail ice. The object next was to reach the other bank, and the attempt was made first to reach this, and then to reach another snag half way, but it was discovered that there was not sufficient rope. Another wagon-bed boat was constructed and sent out with additional rope attached to the desired bank. This actually succeeded in reaching the

Colonel Nelson A. Miles, Fifth U.S. Infantry, whose campaigning in 1876 and 1877 finally ended the war with the Sioux and Cheyennes. Courtesy of Paul L. Hedren.

first one sent to meet it, and the desired juncture was actually effected when the swift current bore down so rapidly that it near capsized the boats, the second of which was so rapidly filling that the rope attached to the north bank had to be loosened and all was again lost. The second boat, however, succeeded in reaching the second snag, thus connecting two-thirds of the river.

Once more a wagon-bed boat was constructed, but could not be made to reach over the nearer snag. It was now progressing towards evening, the party on the raft having been in their narrow prison all day, many having slipped through the interstices in the raft were wet and cold and numb. An abandonment of the enterprise became absolutely necessary, else a night must be passed in the water. To add to the scene now, the river above seemed to have just broken up, for immense ice floes began to sweep down, striking the raft and boat with terrible force, until one immense field of solid ice, covering a third of the river, came booming down the raging current. The outer edge alone struck the raft, while the main body bore down directly upon the men in the boat. The cry to cut the rope arose, but Private [Richard] Bellews [Bellows], of Company "E," calmly untied it, and holding the end until hopeless of longer resisting such force, let go and was borne down without injury by the ice field and this crew soon paddled in to the shore. The huge blocks warned those on the raft that it was high time to do likewise, and drawing in the rope from the opposite bank, the raft was loosened from its snag, the first boat manned, and given one end of this rope, paddled for the shore, while the poles on the raft were vigorously plied. The boat got in to the shore, and the old craft with its thoroughly tired human freight, was hauled in about a quarter of a mile below the scene of their long imprisonment. Terra firma never appeared more agreeable to these before.

Understanding now the full difficulties of the undertaking, but urged by the imperative necessity of making the passage, on the next day, Gen. Miles renewed the attempt to join a rope across, and by going down below to a more narrow point at a rapid bend of the river, the attempt succeeded, and the river was at last spanned by the slender thread. Once more the perils appeared, when Lieut. Baldwin again attempted the passage. Succeeding in crossing, on his return a great field of ice spreading over nearly half the river bore down upon the raft. The men pulled in the rope lustily, but one huge corner struck the raft fairly, and nearly ran over it, covering more than half its space, and placing all in imminent danger of being thrust into the ice-cold foaming current.

From this time on, all the elements seemed to continue against the operations of the command, snowstorms coming in, the river becoming literally filled with floating ice, yet not freezing over, so that though the preparations were continued for a few days, the rations and forage being consumed, the attempt seemed utterly hopeless. A courier too came in [from] Fort Peck, with information that Sitting Bull had gone to the Red Water, a stream midway between Forts Peck and Buford, and scouts also found that the river was frozen over eighteen miles above, at old Fort Hawley, an abandoned [fur trading] post.

Reluctantly, therefore, the intended movement was abandoned. Lieutenant Baldwin with companies "G" and "I," (now commanded by Lieutenant [James H.] Whetton [Whitten], Major [Captain Wyllys] Lyman having been ordered in, sick, from Fort Peck) and "H," (Lieutenant [Frank S.] Hinkle) was ordered to Buford, and also, on his way, to scout the Red Water. Gen. Miles with companies "E" and "A," moved out December 1st for old Fort Hawley. Difficulties were by no means yet at an end, for the march begun over smooth, easy roads, soon became arduous from the broken, ravine-cut country. It was into the late night that the Missouri was again reached. A crossing was effected the next day, an old tumble down dug-out, being taken advantage of to mount the steep bank when at last the dreaded river was passed and the command breathed freely on its southern bank.

Trail still clustered, for before the command rose the

almost perpendicular pine and cedar-covered bluffs. To get up these was an herculean task in accomplishing which twelve mules could scarcely pull up an empty wagon; some had even to be taken apart and carried up the precipitous cliffs. By 10 o'clock at night, however, the labor was accomplished, and the worn out soldiery reposed on the summit of a lofty pine-covered knoll termed "Camp Elevation." Across a deep ravine and a few miles distant were seen bright camp fires, which proved to be Capt. Bennett's, who was on his way back, having performed his required duty.

The country before the present position, attained with such incalculable exertion, was disheartening to behold, yet wondrous and grand in the extreme. Pine-covered peaks, high ridges, cavernous ravines, vertical bluffs spread out in every direction before, while to the northwest the beauteous "Little Rocky Mountains" rose in the blue distance. The Judith and Moccasin mountains to the west sparkled over their snow-clad heights, all presenting a panorama of wild, sublime magnificence. Not to be stayed, on pressed the command, which, by winding along a narrow, rugged "back-bone," found a rude passage down to Crooked creek. All along this day's march, beautiful and graceful deer freely exposed themselves, bounding perchance across the line of march or reposing in the gloomy depths, a prey to the soldier hunter. Down along the tortuous bed of Crooked creek the march continued, Capt. Bennett overtaking and joining the column.

On the next day the command debouched into the wide, forest-covered, grassy bottom of the Musselshell River, where the deer increased to enormous quantities, numbers being slain, yielding rich feasts. But here again difficulties thickened, it being found by a thorough scouting of the country, utterly impossible to proceed up or beyond this stream. The only possible route was found to lay down this river to its entrance into the Missouri, thence along the margin of the latter river to the mouth of Squaw creek. Even greater labor than ever yet performed now arose, for beside the difficulties of the ground, a road had to be cut for one hundred and fifty yards round a point where the high bluff reaches to the swift current of the Missouri, then cut a way up the forty-feet perpendicular bank.

This achieved, the teams had to be taken out, the wagons unloaded and hauled by men, the baggage being carried around and up the bank. A part of this lay over the bordering ice, and the breaking in of the wagons added to the labor. All was done in one day, and on the 6th of December the command passed the scene of its attempted crossing and pushed well up Squaw creek, having at last a practicable road before it. One trial only gave place to another, inasmuch as it was now discovered that the forage had run short, there remaining only enough for four days, complicated by probable storms. "Behind the clouds the sun was still shining," however, for the next day unexpectedly carried the battalion on to the high rolling prairie, and beyond was soon seen the Black Butte, the point where a junction was to be effected with Capt. [Simon] Snyder, commanding the remainder of the Fifth Infantry, and between spread out the wide wooded valley of the Big Dry Fork.

The march now lay over high rolling prairie, smooth and covered with carpet-like buffalo grass. Capt. Snyder's trail was discovered leading into the cantonment, and men were sent in on this with orders to send out forage. Scouts came in and reported Capt. Snyder nearly in. This region over which the rapid march now lay was one of many remarkable features. Generally smooth and rolling like swells of the ocean, off and anon rise loft[y] peaks, buttes of the most variegated shapes, appearing like a multitude of castles dotting the broad expanse. From the summits of these castellated peaks, a measureless view strikes the vision, sweeping over the immense prairie to the blue-black butte, on to the pine-clad hills of the Missouri, on even to the "little rockies" beyond, and eastward to the blue vista of the Yellowstone bluffs.

The difficulties of the command ended, though the sufferings of the animals continued, as by swift marches, the journey proceeded over the divide and down along Sunday creek where forage met and eased the pains of the animals. Thence, two days' march carried the tired, worn, weary, cold and benumbed soldiery into its new, and bleak, and dark, and cheerless, but yet welcome home at Tongue River. Thus, on the 13th of December, ended the remarkable march of this battalion pursuing the arduous tour of its hard duty in this far-off region. . . .

Chapter 12
The Fights at Bark Creek and Ash Creek, December 1876
Frank D. Baldwin

Only Lieutenant Baldwin's battalion engaged Sitting Bull's warriors during the Fort Peck expedition. Ordered by Miles to march to the Fort Peck Agency and investigate rumors of the Hunkpapa leader's presence in that vicinity, Baldwin backtracked with three companies of the Fifth Infantry. Reaching Peck on December 6, Baldwin learned that his quarry was camped on Porcupine Creek east of the agency and north of the Missouri River. By the time the soldiers gained the campsite, Sitting Bull's people had fled toward the Missouri. Baldwin followed and at dawn on December 7 skirmished with the tribesmen as they crossed the ice-packed river opposite the mouth of Bark Creek. Eleven days later Baldwin attacked Sitting Bull's village on Ash Creek, a tributary of Redwater River.

In 1876 thirty-four-year-old Frank D. Baldwin was a seasoned officer, a Michigan veteran of the Civil War who had enlisted in 1861 and had quickly won commission. He fought in numerous battles of the war, joined in Sherman's campaigns in Georgia and the Carolinas, and had been captured and released by the Confederates. On the frontier Baldwin distinguished himself under Miles in the Fifth Infantry, participating in the Red River War of 1874–75 against the Southern Plains tribes. The proud recipient of numerous commendations for gallantry as well as several brevet promotions (in 1891 he would receive two Medals of Honor), Baldwin became a trusted subordinate and often served as Miles's adjutant in the operations of 1876–77. He fought the Sioux several times during the ensuing years and later occupied administrative positions in the military divisions of the Pacific and Missouri. Baldwin served in Cuba and the Philippines during the Spanish-American War and attained the rank of brigadier general before returning to the United States. In 1906 he retired after forty years of service, only to be recalled for a short time during World War I to help train national guardsmen.

First Lieutenant Frank D. Baldwin, Fifth U.S. Infantry. Courtesy of the Kansas State Historical Society, Topeka.

After surviving more than thirty engagements during a career that spanned the Civil War, Indian wars, Spanish-American War, Philippine Insurrection, and World War I, Baldwin died at his home in Denver in 1923.

Baldwin's undated manuscript account of his fights with the Sioux in 1876 reposes in the William Carey Brown Collection of the Western History Collections, Norlin Library, University of

*Colorado. His remembrance begins with the discovery of Sitting
Bull's abandoned camp along Porcupine Creek on December 7,
1876. It is reprinted here with Baldwin's misspellings unchanged.*

WHEN WE FOUND THE ABANDONED CAMP of the Indians
which they had evidently left in great haste as their camp
fires were still burning and much plunder lay scattered
about, we soon found their trail, which was at least 30 yards
wide. The snow was firmly tramped down by them which
made our progress much easier, and we followed it with
much less fatigue. Just before day break several Indians
road up to my pack train and attempted to stampead it but
they were very promptly driven out loosing one of their
number, at least. His body was left on the trail. We at once
moved into a bunch of timber & prepared for action, either
offensive or defensive. It was bitter cold, still it was not safe
to build fires.

As soon as day broke the command moved in line
toward the river which was only a short distance away. We
struck the point where the Indians had just crossed on the
ice. Their rear guard was still on the ice and their long car-
avans of women, children & ponies with packs rushing in
frightened haste could be seen winding their way through
the timbered foothills to the south. Fire was opened on the
retreating Indians, but soon the oposit bank of the river
was lined with their warriors to the number of several hundred. A brisk exchange of shots was continued for two
hours. In the meantime a large number of Yanktonays
[Yanktonais] had gathered in my rear. These Indians were
reputed to be friendly, but we had grave doubts as to this
and I felt obliged to take steps to meet any acts of hostility
on their part which necessitated the withdrawing of one co.
from the front & placing it in my rear, with orders to open
fire on the Yanktonnais if they did not leave at once, which
they had been warned to do & did do in the deployment of
the troops. My line was advanced across the frozen river,

driving the Indians well back, but as soon as their families had gotten well out of range, the warriors commenced to congregate in large numbers.

Taking into consideration that my rear was menaced by the Yanktonays who no doubt would have in some degree participated in the attack had I engaged the openly hostile [Sioux] in my front, which would certainly have required every man I had to hold them in check, I decided to retire across the river, as a defeat with the great river covered with thin ice was liable to break up at any moment & become impassible. This between my command and my base, which would have proven most disastrous in case of defeat. Reaching the north bank of the river without loss, we went into a grove of cotton wood timber & quickly surrounded ourselves with a substantial breastwork composed of logs, where I felt secure for a time at least against all the Indians of the country. My men were greatly exhausted with the excessive cold & lack of sleep or rest. Fires were built, food prepared, one half of the command on duty under arms at all times, while the other half were sleeping. All day the hostiles were in sight after venturing so close that they were in fairly good range when shots were exchanged.

As the day advanced, the Ther[mometer] went lower & lower & by the middle of the after noon a furious blizzard was on, coming from the west. About five o'clock the Indians had entirely disapeared. Our worst enemy, the blizzard, was increasing its fury. My men were not prepared to withstand it very long without ample food & protection. I had learned from past experience that these severe storms lasted from three to five days without cessation. I decided to return to Fort Peck. After preparing & consumed all the food that remained, the packs were adjusted and we started on our return tramp, satisfied with the results of our efforts, as we had driven the Indians out of their winter camp at the most inclement season of the year. The suffering of the troops, although great, could in no way be compaired with that of the Indians, including that of the women & children.

With the pack trains in the lead to break the trail, the raging storm in our faces, the march was necessarily slow, the men began to get numb and some of them more or less listless[s], which caused drowsiness, and it was not long before they would through [throw] themselves into the snow, sound asleep. Any of you who have ever been at the point of freezing will realize that these were your sensations and feelings. This was a condition that must be met & overcome. We were on the great plains, no shelter or fuel available. The men once down could not be arroused by simple shaking or draging him. Hence six or eight of the strongest men of the command were selected & with fixed bayonets place[d] in the rear, an officer in rear of each co., with orders that if a man laid down he was to be probed with the bayonet. If he did not move instantly, when spoken to, these orders were effectively carried out. A long rope was attached to a mule and strung out to the rear. The men took hold of this and would hang on like grim death. Occasionally the mule would be put to a slow trot, the men holding on to the rope would have to increase their gait which caused a quicker pulsation of the blood, this of course was beneficial.

Overcoming these trying conditions, the command reached Fort Peck at 7 A.M. the ninth [midday Dec. 8], with no other damage than frozen ears, fingers, and feet. Fifty-seven men of the command were treated for these causes at the hospital. As an example of the character of the well disciplined & thoroughly trained soldiers, we will give an instants, following this the most trying, hazerdous & exacting experience of my life. I had sent a mounted man on to the fort directing that breakfast should be prepared for my men. It was in readiness as soon as the men could lay off their equipments & through [throw] out a little.

After consuming this bountiful and well prepared meal the men were turned loose on the carcas[s] of a large Buffalo which had been killed near the camp the day before. This was entirely consumed by noon, when they quite contentedly took to their blankets & slept until supper time. The mercurial Ther had frozen up during the night, but the spirit Ther registered 42° & better below zero, a little chilling for an 18 mile night march through the snow.

To allow my men to recover somewhat from their extraordinary exposure of the past two days, I was obliged to remain at Fort Peck some time. I could learn nothing definite as to the point to which the hostiles had retreated, still I felt sure they had gone south and would probably establish themselves on some one of the southern tributaries of the Mo. river, and as the Redwater presented the most favorable conditions on account of timber I decided to make the head of this tributary my next objective field of operations. Repairing the transportation, gathering a supply of buffalo meat, we remained in camp three days. On the fourth day started with the entire outfit down the left bank of the river following the main road toward Fort Buford, hoping to misleading the Indians as to my intentions. We marched to Wolf Point, several miles further east than was necessary and some miles below the mouth of Redwater Cr. Here I remained one day, having secured the services of two excellent scouts, Culbertson & Lambert.

I left Wolf Point at nightfull with 3 sacks of grain for 150 animals and three days rations for the men. We were entering a country wholly unknown in the midst of winter and without any delay it was at least five days marching to our cantonment (Tongue river). Before leaving Fort Peck I had sent by couriers a request to the cantonment that supplies be sent down the Yellowstone to meet me. In crossed [crossing] the Mo river had to unhitch the teams & drop [drag] the wagons across on account of the thin ice,

accomplishing the crossing successfully. We moved up
Wolf cr. for a few miles then crossed a small divide to the
westward into the valley of Redwater. There we haulted a
few hours for rest. The snow was so deep that often we
were obliged to dig our way through heavy drifts, which
delayed our progress and added an unusual amount of
fatigue to both men & animals. After a few hours rest in this
our first camp on the Redwater Cr., we again started moving up the valley until dark, when [we] camp for the night
and allowing small fires to be built.

At day break the following morning, Dec. 18, 1876,
found us again on the move floundering through snow,
carefully holding to the valley so as to not expose our
whereabouts. About one oclock as we were nearing the
head of Redwater Cr. [actually a tributary of the Redwater
called Ash Creek] and the bluffs which was the divide
between the Yellowstone & the Mo. river an Indian
mounted was discovered in our front, and shortly thereafter smoke was plainly seen raising from the Indian camp
not more than two miles away. Had we been mounted, a
few moments would have found the command in the Indian
camp. Scarcely slackening our pace, the trains closed up
forming in four columns, the infy in line, one co. in front &
one on each flank with a small guard in rear. We moved forward as rapidly as possible direct for the camp, which was
soon attacked, the Indians driven out thoroughly stampeded leaving quantities of plunder. The camp consisted of
122 lodges, many of which were left standing, sixty head of
stock, Buffalo roabs & meat in large quantities & nearly
every kind of supplies as usually issued at their agencies,
such as sugar, tea, flour, calico, red cloth blankets &c were
found in this camp & fell into our hands, and such as could
be made useful was loaded into the wagons, the balance
was distroied.

I will here mention an instants that demonstrated the
esprit which invaded the minds of my men. From causes

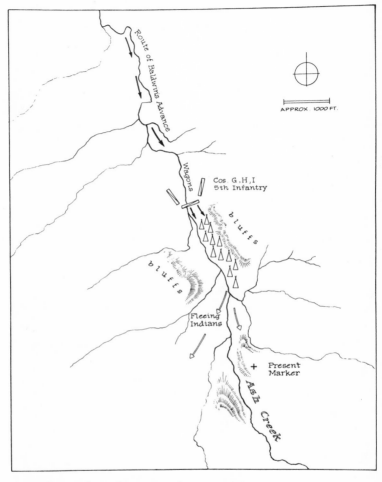

The Ash Creek Fight, December 18, 1876.

incident to the campaign there was nearly forty of the men
riding in the wagons not being able to endure the fatigue of
keeping in the ranks. When the order for formation for
attack was given there was not one of those men that did

not join his company, & struggling along as best he could remained there until the affair was settled. My camp for the night was made near that just- vacated by the hostiles. We had secured an abundance of food & hundreds of Robes & blankets, each man utilizing what he wanted for his comfort, enough being left so that each animal had a covering, and for once every man and beast was comfortable despite the fact that the Ther. registered 40° & more degrees below zero. Subsequently, these robes & blankets were distributed among the men & were made up into garments & sleeping bags of some sort and added greatly to the comfort of all.

The next morning camp was broken & the march was continued over the divide & down into the valley of the Yellowstone, where [we] haulted for the night. The Indians had hovered about our camp all last night & on our flanks all day. Just before sun set the camp was attacked quite vigorously but the Indians were quickly driven away. From this camp I sent a courier to the cantonment reporting my where abouts &c, &c, and saying that we had an abundance of rations, in fact, everything but forage and it would not be necessary to send our supplies but the train had already started which we met about noon the following day, loaded with good eatables & sundries for both men & beasts. Also a note from Genl Miles in part as follows "I am delighted to learn that you have been successful in your engagement & without loss. I sent Capt [Ezra P.] Ewers out with supplies for you. I want to see you as soon as you can get near enough. Take what mounted men you want and come in in the night."

As soon as we had gotten comfortably supplied with food &c, after dusk I mounted my famos horse "Red Water," which had carried me night and day more than 300 miles during this the most severe & exhausting as well as exacting campaign considering its short duration, that I had ever experienced. Accompanied by mounted men, · [I] started for the cantonment about 30 miles distant, arriving at 2 in the morning, Dec. 21st 1876, when I was greeted by a most hearty and gratifying reception. We had not only kept the Indians moving, but had had two spirited encounters & destroied & captured large quantities of their supplies & some of them were killed.

Chapter 13

The Crook-Mackenzie Campaign and the Dull Knife Battle, November 25, 1876

Henry H. Bellas

During the period that Colonel Miles's infantry soldiers were tramping through Montana snowdrifts going to and from Fort Peck on the Missouri River, General Crook was beginning a new offensive against Crazy Horse's followers far to the south. Crook, with Colonel Ranald S. Mackenzie's cavalrymen, together with infantry and artillery troops, embarked from Fort Fetterman on November 14 and traveled north via Cantonment Reno. Learning of the proximity of a large camp of Northern Cheyennes sheltered along the Red Fork of Powder River in the fastness of the Big Horn Mountains, Crook directed Mackenzie forward. The victory of Mackenzie's soldiers over Chief Dull Knife's Cheyennes was one of the biggest of the war. It was also fraught with significance, for the battle ended major Cheyenne participation in the conflict while forcing refugees from the Red Fork village to seek succor with Crazy Horse in the Tongue River region below the Yellowstone—in effect producing more Indians for Miles to contend with.

Henry H. Bellas penned the following account of the Crook-Mackenzie campaign and the Dull Knife Fight of November 25, 1876, some twenty years after the event. A Pennsylvanian by birth, Bellas had been appointed second lieutenant in the Fourth Cavalry in 1873 and spent the following three years fighting Indians in Texas, the Indian Territory, Kansas, Nebraska, and Wyoming. The strenuous western service ruined his health, and in 1886 he retired as a first lieutenant because of disabilities incurred in the line of duty. Bellas's essay on the Crook-Mackenzie winter initiative, which appeared in Recreation 6 *(February 1897), details his regiment's mobilization and participation in rounding up agency Indians as well as the expedition and the resulting battle.*

[FOLLOWING THE LITTLE BIG HORN DISASTER,] orders were issued for the transfer of troops from all the other departments to the scene of conflict, to prevent a general uprising over the entire western country. Our regiment, the 6th [4th] Cavalry, then on duty in the panhandle of Texas and in the Indian Territory [present Oklahoma], was one of the first called for, and was soon en route to the Department of the Platte.

My troop had but recently returned to its post—Fort Elliott—from a summer scout on the Staked Plains and on the occurrence of the outbreak had been first ordered to change station to Fort Dodge, Kansas, 200 miles farther North.

Early the next morning I was on the march for my new station. After crossing the Canadian and while in camp on Commission creek, late one evening, a courier rode into our camp with the news of the Custer massacre and with despatches from department headquarters directing the different troop commanders to proceed as rapidly as possible, and, on reaching the railroad, to ship their commands immediately for the North.

Three or 4 days later I arrived at Fort Dodge, and after drawing supplies for the journey, transferred my troop to the cars and started for the Department of the Platte, via Las Animas, Denver and Cheyenne. From the latter point, I took up the march again, by way of Forts Russell and Laramie, for Red Cloud Agency, in Nebraska, some 200 miles farther to the northward. My troop was one of the first to reach the agency, but soon after, companies and battalions of all arms of the service, from East, West and South, began to arrive at the rendezvous. General Crook had taken the field, in the summer, with [Colonel Wesley] Merritt's column of cavalry, and this force, after varied successes and many privations, took up its return march for the agency in October, leaving the hostile Sioux still in large force and in comparative possession of the entire

Black Hills country, as well as that lying toward the Big Horn mountains and the Yellowstone. An expedition against them in the dead of winter, when hampered in their movements for want of grazing for their stock, was seen to be the only way to reach the hostiles effectively, provided we could subsist our own column in the meantime. It was also evident that we should be out the greater portion of the winter, and it was deemed advisable not only to make careful preparations for the safety and proper equipment of the expedition, but also to provide comfortable quarters for the troops, on their return.

The large bodies of recruits now arriving were accordingly drilled 3 times daily; while the entire force was at the same time set to work cutting, hauling and sawing logs and building rude barracks and stables for the command. These preparations continued steadily until the beginning of November, exciting the interest of the thousands of semi-friendly Indians still surrounding the agency. They watched all our movements, noted the arrival of every new body of troops and no doubt continually reported, by runners, every item of news to their friends who were still out from the reservations. Furthermore they furnished these renegades with supplies of provisions and arms. These communications were continued so regularly, notwithstanding several arrests made by us at the agency, that it was determined by Generals Crook and [Colonel] Mackenzie—the latter being in command of the cavalry column of the expedition now organizing—to send, as a preparatory measure, the whole force of cavalry against these Indians, who had established a sort of half-way station between the agency and the hostiles' camps.

Accordingly, on the evening of October 22d, 6 squadrons of picked men and horses—each over 150 strong—started, quietly, about 9 o'clock, for an all night's ride to surround the camps of the Sioux chiefs Red Cloud and Red Leaf, some 40 miles north from the agency. Our orders were to capture and bring both bands back to their reservation, where they could be under the surveillance of the military. Only one day's rations were taken and no baggage of any kind—the whole command being in light marching order. The night was pitch-dark and very cold. The country was intersected by a series of ravines and washouts; but the most positive orders having been issued by Mackenzie, who was in command, for the whole column to keep closed up, at all hazards, the trot and gallop were continued throughout the night. Occasionally a troop would be brought down to a walk, at the bottom of some gully or dry creek, and then, on emerging, would be compelled to go at a gallop to overtake the preceding troops, which had already disappeared in the blackness ahead.

The only sounds to be heard were the thunder of the column as it tore along over the frozen ground; the rattle of the harness of the horses (the men's sabres being thrust between their knees and saddles) and the muttered exclamation of some trooper as his steed stumbled or fell in the darkness. Such riding was of course terribly fatiguing to both horses and riders. The men always regarded a night ride as far worse than a week's ordinary march. Experience, however, had taught us, as well as our gallant commander, that it was the only sure way "to catch the weasel asleep."

By the gray light of the morning, we found ourselves cautiously and slowly approaching the two camps of sleeping Indians. One battalion, under Colonel [Major George A.] G——[Gordon, Fifth Cavalry], had been sent to surround Red Leaf's band; the other, under Major [Captain Clarence] M——[Mauck, Fourth Cavalry], that of Red Cloud; the 2 bands being encamped about 2 miles apart. In each case the result was the same. As the different troops swung quickly and successively into their positions, the watchful dogs of the camps gave the alarm. The Indians,

Colonel Ranald S. Mackenzie, Fourth U.S. Cavalry, whose command attacked Dull Knife's village on November 25, 1876. Courtesy of the Nebraska State Historical Society, Lincoln.

completely surprised, sprang to their arms. A rapid fusillade followed. There was a rush and a shout from the troops, and the next moment we were in possession of both camps and all, or nearly all, of their inhabitants were our prisoners, escape being almost impossible.

They were at once ordered to surrender their weapons, pack up their lodges and all their effects and move with their herds—which were afterward to be taken from them—into the agency. This order was only complied with after many of their unpacked possessions had been committed to the flames, accompanied by the chanting of the savage "death-song."

We had little time to eat or rest, as the return march was soon taken up. By dark we had made about one-half the distance to the agency. To prevent escape, the General [Colonel Mackenzie] determined to send the bucks, numbering over 100, on into the post that same night, leaving the rest of the column, with the women and children, to await rations and to slowly make their way in the next day.

Four troops, including my own, were accordingly selected and under the command of Colonel Gordon, started with the captive Indians in the centre of the column—2 being mounted on each pony. The trot was at once taken up and continued the whole remaining distance. By 11 o'clock our destination was reached and the outfit, including Red Cloud and Red Leaf themselves, safely secured in one of the warehouses of the post.

The work of our battalion was over for the time. A ride of 90 miles or more, with the surround and capture of 2 large Indians encampments, in a little over 24 hours, was certainly lively work and gave strong evidence that the comparatively raw recruits, composing full half the command, might be depended on in the approaching winter campaign.

All being in readiness, the Power River Expedition— which was so named by reason of its supposed ultimate destination—started, on the first day of November, on its long and dreary march toward that inhospitable region. The force consisted of 6 squadrons of cavalry, under Mackenzie, one battalion of heavy artillery and 3 large battalions of infantry under Colonel [Lieutenant Colonel Richard I.] Dodge. We had also a pack train of 400 mules, in charge of experienced packers, and a long ambulance and wagon train. There were altogether over 2,500 men. Accompanying the expedition, in the capacity of guides and scouts, and under the command of officers selected from the cavalry, was a body of 100 friendly Indians—Pawnees, Arapahoes, Crows, Bannocks, Shoshones, Snakes, and even Sioux and Cheyennes; for any Indian will betray even those of his own tribe, including all his wife's relations, provided the reward offered be sufficiently tempting.

The march, for a distance of 15 miles, was through the White river canyon—a dangerous pass leading from the agency—thence northward through the sandhills of Wyoming via Forts Laramie and Fetterman (crossing the Platte twice) toward the head of the Powder river in the Big Horn mountains. At the last named post, General Crook, with his staff, overtook and assumed command of the expedition.

A week later, Fort Reno, an old abandoned post on the Powder river, was reached, and while here intelligence was brought by one of our Indians scouts of the proximity of a small party of hostile Cheyennes—some 4 or 5 lodges—encamped but a few miles to the West of us. Our scouts were sent out a second time and captured one of the band. He had ridden into the camp of our allies, in the evening, supposing them to be friends, and only discovered his mistake after he had informed them of the location of the main body of the Cheyennes, in the canyon at the head of one branch of the Powder river and on the opposite or western side of the Big Horn mountains. He also told of the encampment of the Sioux, under Crazy Horse, still farther to the north on the Rosebud [Tongue River].

Then, suddenly, he found himself in the midst of foes and a prisoner, as the party covered him with carbines and revolvers and compelled him to surrender his arms. He was immediately brought in to headquarters, closely guarded; and though now obstinate and sullen, enough was elicited from him to corroborate his previous unwary confession.

Orders were at once issued by Crook to prepare for a 10 days' rapid march, with the pack train only, toward Crazy Horse's camp, to strike a decisive blow at the main body of hostile Sioux encamped there. The expedition proceeded as rapidly as the snow would allow—for it had been storming heavily for the past week or more, with the thermometer falling far below the freezing point. The character of the country had likewise become not only much rougher but more bleak and desolate. There was no timber save in the creek bottoms, while the prairie, like the steppes of Tartary, was but a vast desert of sands hills, covered with the despised sage brush and dwarf cactus. Not a sign of game was seen, save an occasional sage hen, as the long column kept on its way, day after day, still northward toward Cloud Peak, now clearly seen, though 80 miles away, rising majestically upward like a huge mass of white clouds in the clear sky.

On reaching Crazy Woman's Fork of the north branch of the Powder river, after a long day's march, Sitting Bear, one of our scouts, who had been far ahead of the column and near Crazy Horse's camp, brought back word that the small band of Cheyennes, already missing their comrade, had been likewise scouting the country, and observing our column, as well as the direction it was taking, had immediately divined its destination. Hastily decamping, they had hurried in advance, passing Sitting Bear on their way, toward the encampment of Crazy Horse, to give the alarm, and most likely to cause the retreat of the whole tribe.

The course of their trail indicated this and perceiving that our expedition, in that direction, was defeated, but that they had probably not sent any warning to the large Cheyenne camp on the opposite side of the Big Horns, which was now in our rear, Crook immediately countermanded his orders and quietly reversed the march of the expedition.

On the evening of November 23d the infantry and artillery were left in charge of the wagon trains and the whole body of cavalry—12 troops, each nearly 100 strong—started, under Mackenzie, for a rapid ride across the mountains, to strike the Cheyennes under Dull Knife. A number of our Indian allies were, as usual, sent ahead, through the passes, to locate the hostile camp, while the others remained to guide the column. The march was resumed at sunrise. By noon the scouts reached a grassy vale, completely sheltered from observation in front, by a semicircular range of hills. Here they halted to allow the cavalry to come up.

On its arrival, and just as the pack train was going into camp here, the Indian outposts were suddenly seen to commence circling around, with their ponies at full gallop, in a wild and excited manner. The next moment a shrill yell went up from the scout stationed farthest to the front. Supposing we were about to be attacked, the whole command, in less time than it takes to tell it, was in line and rushing forward to the brow of the range of hills, with skirmishers thrown out in advance. The cause of the alarm was now ascertained to be the return of some of the Indian scouts sent out the preceding evening to locate the exact position of the hostile camp. They had communicated their discovery of us by signals, on seeing our outposts, while the howling of our allies, stationed as sentries, was but a shout of triumph at the return of the others. When these arrived at our headquarters—so worn out that their ponies fell exhausted and the riders were in almost as bad a plight—

we ascertained that the village was still some distance ahead; though how far was difficult to say; as an Indian's ideas of time and distance are rather indefinite. Mackenzie, however, thought it possible, by making an all night ride, to strike the hostile village by daybreak in the morning. After a few hours' rest and a cheerless meal of hardtack and cold bacon—no fires being now allowed—the command again started, with the pack train to follow under escort of a detachment 2 hours later. Emerging from the basin in which we had halted, we entered a wild pass, through the red sandstone cliffs, and then clambered up and over a second hill, which commanded a full view of the entire column stretched out far behind. The next instant the scene vanished at the head of the column, as it began the descent in front.

All through the cold, dark night was the march persistently continued; with little or no halting, but with our scouts always thrown far in advance; over jagged hills, then cautiously winding around their sides, on narrow ledges and overlooking deep, yawning chasms below; then crawling down, in single file and dismounted, into dark ravines, across rapid or miry mountain streams and then up and out over the hills again.

Once we passed through a beautiful level valley, about 3 miles long by half a mile wide, which the men nicknamed the "racecourse," and where the gallop was quickly taken up and continued throughout its whole length. By the gray dawn of the coming morning, 25 miles had been covered. Had it been possible for us to proceed in a straight line, less than one-half that distance would have been necessary.

As we approached the mouth of the canyon in which lay the hostile encampment, the country became constantly rougher, being more and more intersected with ravines running in every direction, and several of the horses of the column fell exhausted and dying. The beating of war drums and the yelling of the Cheyennes were now distinctly heard. Familiar sounds they were, to most of us; but our scouts soon returned from a reconnaissance of the camp to assure us that this demonstration had not been occasioned by our coming, but was probably a celebration of the massacre of some venturesome miners, or of a band of Indians belonging to a hostile tribe.

Orders were at once given to prepare for a charge. The long column was closed up as compactly as possible, while our Indian allies commenced casting off all superfluous clothing and all extra weight from their ponies. Then, gayly decked out for the occasion, they pressed eagerly to the front, like race horses coming to the score. The battalion under Colonel Gordon led the advance, while Major Mauck's followed directly after. The Indians [allies] swarmed in front, and on either flank, surrounding the general and his staff, at the head of the leading battalion.

Replying to the clear notes of the bugle, as it rang out the charge—echoed and reechoed from the walls of the canyon—was the music furnished by one of the Pawnees, who sounded a wild humming tune on a pipe that rose above all other sounds and somewhat resembled the prolonged shriek of a steam whistle. Added to this were now the shouts and cries of our foremost line of scouts, who dashed into the herds of ponies to stampede them. Then quickly followed a few sharp flashes from rifle, carbine and pistol, in the dim morning light, the loud cheer of our troopers and the thundering roar of more than 1,200 horsemen of the rushing column resounding from the sides of the narrow canyon.

This canyon, it should be here stated, is about 4 miles long and from a quarter of a mile to a mile in width, with the clear headwaters of the North Fork of Powder river flowing through it, from west to east. The lodges of the village were on both sides of the stream and numbered over

200; so that, allowing 5 persons (the average) to a tepee, the total population was close to 1,000. A little plateau ran parallel to the stream and lodges, for nearly a mile on the north side of the canyon, and terminated, at the western end, in a high red sandstone butte that commanded the whole village. Beyond this huge mound the canyon closed in a series of low, flat-topped hills, much cut up with ravines, to which many of the Cheyennes fled as they saw us entering at the opposite end.

As the leading troops came dashing up the canyon, the remainder of the tribe, alarmed by the noise of the rapidly advancing column and cut short in their war song and dance, by the stern reality of war, started at first to defend their encampment; but the next moment, realizing the hopelessness of such an effort, retreated rapidly to the foothills beyond. Our column, after charging through the village, seized a commanding position on the red butte, as well as on the tops of several other bluffs 400 to 500 feet high, on the sides of and overlooking the canyon. Then they started forward to dislodge the hostiles from the ravines in front.

Lieutenant [John A.] McKinney, dashing fearlessly forward at the head of his troop, was met at the end of the canyon with a volley from the concealed foe ahead. Rider and horse both fell, mortally wounded by half a dozen bullets, while the leading fours of the troop were shot down at the same time. The men, thrown into confusion and unable to advance across the ravines, hesitated for a moment; but quickly reforming, under their remaining officer, as another troop swept by them to the front, again charged forward against these formidable natural intrenchments. The enemy in their front was now speedily dislodged and destroyed; but as the troops continued to crowd into the canyon, they were placed at a great disadvantage, being exposed to the fire of the hostiles who were comparatively secure from observation.

Many of the men and horses fell, from the hidden fire poured in on them from the hills at the West end of the canyon as they endeavored to cross the little plateau overlooking the village. I was twice afterward, as I rode rapidly across the plain, honored with special volleys; but in both cases I escaped unharmed.

Broad daylight now succeeding the gray dawn which had prevailed when the attack commenced, the troops were dismounted, the horses led back behind the butte and the enemy quickly driven out, in succession, from one ravine after another, till completely beyond the range of our carbines.

They now resorted to strategy, endeavoring to draw our men out from their shelter by springing boldly up in view, confident of their own safety in being supplied with weapons superior in range to our own. Then they would suddenly pour in a volley with deadly effect. Their fire, however, slacked, toward noon, and we soon understood the reason; large quantities of ammunition being discovered in the tepees, from which we had driven the hostiles.

Our Indian allies, who had in the meantime fought, recklessly, beside the soldiers, against their own race, now taking advantage of the lull in the fight, returned to the village and, having already secured the main herds, commenced to plunder the encampment from one end to another. One or two squaws were found secreted in the lodges, unable to escape, and now refusing to come out and surrender were, in spite of the remonstrances of the soldiers, quickly shot and scalped. The tepees were filled with large quantities of dried meat and skins, blankets and cooking utensils. The kettles all had water in them and the fires were burning, as if in preparation for the morning meal. All regrets, if any existed, for the destruction of the encampment vanished, as many relics of the ill-fated Custer expedition now came to view. Silk guidons, officers' blouses and overcoats, a jaunty buckskin coat with a bullet-hole in the shoulder (supposed to be the one worn by Tom Custer—the brother of the general—in the Little Big Horn fight), hats, caps, gauntlets, sabres, watches, pocket-books (with money in them), target-practice and memorandum books, rosters of the different troops of the Seventh Cavalry, curry-combs, bridles, saddles, canteens, etc., all in the greatest profusion, were found everywhere. In the herds were also several horses branded with the troop letter and the regimental number; while, among the Indian trophies were found several fresh scalps, which were identified by our Bannocks and Shoshones as evidence of the massacre of members of their tribes across the mountains. These accounted for the war song and dance we had so rudely interrupted that morning. Several beaded necklaces, decorated with dried human fingers—one having 10 others 5, 6, or 8 of these horrible mementoes—were likewise found and identified by our furious allies.

Many of the troops were now withdrawn behind the butte, to get a few moments' rest and a bite to eat, having been fasting for nearly 24 hours. The pack train, which had come up during the fight, in the morning, and had been parked in the willows, during the day, was unloaded for the first time since the preceding afternoon. The horses were already gathered here, as also were the wounded men, who were being carefully cared for by the surgeons accompanying the expedition.

Throughout the afternoon the fight was kept up. Mackenzie endeavored to dislodge the hostiles from their last stronghold with as little loss as possible from their sharpshooters. A direct charge on their position would not have compensated us for the loss we should have necessarily sustained. Finally, toward sundown, they withdrew from our front some 5 or 6 miles, completely beaten. All our dead were now brought in, while our allies secured many scalps from their fallen foes whom the Cheyennes had been unable to carry off with them. They paraded these trophies

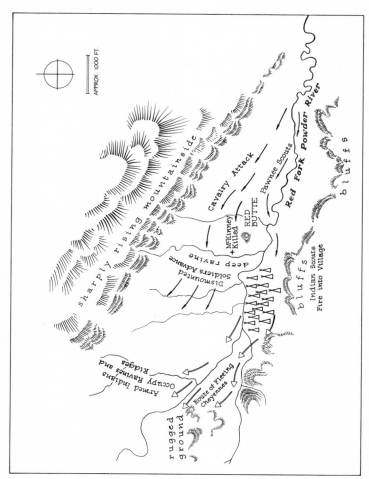

The Dull Knife Battle, November 25, 1876.

about our camp fires, in the evening, with the greatest glee.

Our loss we ascertained to be one officer killed (Lieutenant McK——) in whose honor a military post was afterward named, by order of the War Department. Two other officers were struck with spent balls, while between 30 and 40 enlisted men and 2 of our Indian scouts were killed or wounded, besides a number of our horses.

Nearly 100 of the enemy had been killed or wounded, 3 of Dull Knife's sons being among the dead. That night both sides slept upon their arms, in anticipation of an attack, but none was made. The Cheyennes were compelled to kill several of their remaining ponies for food, but they refused all suggestions of surrender, being now desperate.

Preparations were accordingly made for renewing the fight early the next morning; but our foes, taking advantage of a heavy snow storm that had set in, secretly decamped and started across the mountains to make their way to the encampment of the Sioux under Crazy Horse. It was impossible for us to follow with our horses, and as we were encumbered with our wounded, Mackenzie determined to return to the supply camp, where we had left the artillery and infantry with the wagon train.

All our dead and wounded were placed on *travois*— litters made out of lodge poles having one end hitched to a mule, while the other dragged on the ground—and the column started on its return march. Before leaving, however, the hostile village—or what was left of it—with its contents was given to the flames. Over 600 head of ponies had been captured and after the distribution among our Indian scouts had been made, all those remaining, and not worth keeping, were shot, to prevent their recapture.

The return march occupied about twice the time of the advance. The whole route over which the command had passed during the night preceding the fight, was found strewn with all kinds of clothing and horse equipments; proof of the hard ride we had made to accomplish our purpose.

In just one week after our departure from our supply camp we returned to it, completely successful; though had a smaller force attacked this same Indian encampment, situated as it was, not one of the command, it is believed, would have returned to tell of it, and the Custer massacre would have been duplicated.

The next day the last sad rites were held over the dead—numbering now a dozen, as several of the wounded had since died. All were committed to one large grave; a rude monument of rocks being raised above their resting place. Lieutenant McK——'s remains were sent, under escort, over our former route, toward the railroad, for shipment to his family in the States. All the wounded, as well as those officers and men who had already succumbed to the hardships of the campaign and severe weather, were at the same time sent into Fort Fetterman, while the remainder of the column soon after started across to the Black Hills country, in order to head off Crazy Horse, who it was supposed had retreated eastward across the Powder river toward that region.

Following down the Belle Fourche or north fork of the Cheyenne river, which encircles the Black Hills, we found the country, after leaving old Fort Reno, more desolate and destitute of grazing than ever. Bare buttes rose here and there over the bleak plains, the only timber being the young cotton woods and willows fringing the river banks. The former we used, when possible, for firewood, feeding our animals on the bark and twigs. Often no fuel was to be found but the miserable sage brush, the roots of which were used to make a smoky fire that lasted only a few minutes. Still, such fires were kept up, by reliefs, all through the night, replenishing them constantly, to keep us from freezing in our beds of snow. Three or 4 of us, combining robes and blankets, generally "turned in" together for the night, equipped in overcoats, hats and boots—disrobing being out of the question, as we were frequently destitute of both fire and tents during our winter campaign. The former were often forbidden or impossible, while we were unable to transport the latter, by packs, when separated from the trains.

The thermometer, on Christmas morning, stood at 40° below zero. How much lower the temperature fell the surgeons were unable to report, as the mercury froze in the bulb. Frozen noses, fingers and feet were general. The old buffalo robes which we had taken from the Cheyenne village, were cut up and made into shoes, leggings and caps, to afford protection from this truly Arctic weather. "Sundogs," which occur only in an extremely low temperature, were frequently visible. Iron tent pins or picket pins, were abandoned in the frozen ground, where driven, and water was only to be had by cutting holes in the ice. Our horses soon learned to kneel, in line, and thrust their noses through these openings to drink. The only use we had for water was for making coffee, which, with hard-tack and raw, frozen bacon often constituted, for days, our sole subsistence.

The horses and mules commenced to give way, even more rapidly than the men, under this exposure and the loss of their forage, though the cavalry relieved their animals, as far as possible, by dismounting and walking more or less. A dozen or more horses gave out each day of our journey. These were shot, by the guard stationed at the rear of the column, to prevent their falling into the hands of the hostile Indians, who in small bands hovered around us. This fact we were made unpleasantly aware of by the stampeding of the horses of several of the troops, at night. These were fortunately recovered, having run into other portions of the camp. These marauders also killed and scalped several destitute miners and prospectors, who incautiously strayed a mile or 2 from our column which they had joined and followed for some time, for safety. It would have been a useless wearing out of our already weak horses to have pursued these small bands, over this bleak and snow-covered desert. Additional orders were therefore issued to prevent straggling—many of the cavalry being now afoot and frequently falling out to rest and rejoin other portions of the command.

As we now finally neared Deadwood, without finding indications of any large body of hostile Sioux—Crazy Horse having retreated still farther Northward, across the Yellowstone [sic]—General Crook resolved to proceed to Red Cloud Agency again, in order to recuperate men and animals during the remainder of the winter and to prepare for the spring campaign, as well as to be ready for any emergency that might arise. The return march was accordingly taken up and, proceeding southward, the entire column recrossed the Platte river on the ice. By the end of January the whole command had arrived at the termination of its winter's journey, of over 1,000 miles. . . .

Chapter 14

The Wolf Mountains Expedition and the Battle of Wolf Mountains, January 8, 1877

Henry R. Tilton and Edmond Butler

On December 16 an important event occurred near the Tongue River cantonment. As five Sioux headmen from Crazy Horse's village advanced on the post to ascertain chances for a peaceful settlement of the conflict, they were suddenly attacked by the army's Crow Indian scouts. All the Sioux were killed before soldiers rushing from the garrison could save them. The episode ruined any prospect for a peaceful outcome to the war.

Miles had to go after Crazy Horse. His final major movement in the Great Sioux War was his strike against the Sioux and Northern Cheyennes far up Tongue River valley from the cantonment. Crazy Horse had camped for the winter along the stream's headwaters, where his force had been augmented in early December by the arrival of Cheyenne survivors of the fight on the Red Fork of the Powder. Miles's expedition of December 1876–January 1877 succeeded in besting the tribesmen in an important encounter in the Wolf Mountains fought on January 8, 1877.

Two accounts follow. That of Henry R. Tilton provides immediate perspective by an army doctor of the overall expedition as well as important commentary on the travails of winter campaigning. That of Captain Edmond Butler affords a detailed rendering of the battle action from the viewpoint of a company commander. Tilton was born in 1836 in New Jersey and graduated from the University of Pennsylvania medical department in 1859. He served as an assistant surgeon (first lieutenant) at various federal hospitals in the South during the Civil War, after which he was posted to the trans-Mississippi frontier. Tilton accompanied several Indian campaigns, including the 1873 Yellowstone expedition, and was advanced to the grade of major and surgeon in 1876. Following the Sioux War, he helped Miles prosecute the Nez Percés, winning a Medal of Honor for conspicuous bravery at Bear Paw Mountains, Montana. After continuing his work in the medical department, Tilton retired from the army a lieutenant colonel in 1900.

Edmond Butler, a native of Ireland, was forty-nine years old when he led Company C in combat at Wolf Mountains. He had served as an officer with the Fifth Infantry since 1861, and during the Civil War he was stationed variously in Kansas, New Mexico, and Texas, campaigning extensively with his regiment against Indians. He participated in the Red River War under Miles, then joined that officer in prosecuting the Teton Sioux, Northern Cheyennes, and Nez Percés on the Northern Plains. Butler also held numerous staff positions during his thirty-year military career, which ultimately saw him promoted to lieutenant colonel in 1891. For his action at Wolf Mountains, Butler received a brevet of major and a Medal of Honor. He died in retirement in 1895.

Tilton's account of the Wolf Mountains expedition is located in the National Archives, Record Group 94, Records of the Adjutant General's Office.

I HAVE THE HONOR TO REPORT that an expedition was organized at this [Tongue River] Cantonment for operations against hostile Indians. The troops consisted of Cos. A, C, D, E, and K, 5th Infantry and E & F, 22nd Infantry, each company being increased to 58 men by details from the companies which were to remain at the post. There was a small mounted party of enlisted men and 5 white and 6 Indian scouts. Cos. E & F, 22nd Infantry, and D, 5th Infantry, left the post Dec. 27th 1876 attended by Asst. Surg. L. S. Tesson, U.S.A., Capt. [Charles J.] Dickey, 22nd Infantry, in command. Besides the company wagons there were four wagons heavily loaded with supplies drawn by oxen. [On] December 28th Capt. M. Carter with Co K, 5th Infantry, joined Capt. Dickey. [On] December 29th Genl [Colonel] Miles and staff with Cos. A, C, & E, 5th Infantry, and a small supply train started on the same trail. It was in the midst of a snow storm and the thermometer was at −10°. On two or three occasions cattle had been stolen

Surgeon Henry R. Tilton, Fifth U.S. Infantry. Courtesy of the National Library of Medicine, Bethesda, Maryland.

from the beef contractor and the trail followed up the valley of Tongue River.

The scouts with Capt. Dickey recaptured 108 head the second day out: 4 Indians were driving the stock. Orders had been given while at the post to provide 4 wall tents for the accomodation of 8 officers at Hd Qrs. 3 of these were in original packages and at our first camp upon opening the boxes we found that our shelter for the trip was to be linen tents. On the 31st we overtook Capt. Dickey's Battalion. Our progress was not very rapid as the snow was from 6 to 8 inches deep, making the marching difficult. On this day's march the remains of several cattle were found, showing that we were on the right track.

[On] January 1st at the close of the day's march, the scouts met the first hostile Indians about 55 miles from the Cantonment. On the 3rd of January an alarm was given. It proved to be caused by a party of about 20 Indians dashing through camp after the rear-guard had left it. 4 men of the mounted party with one or more citizens were back looking for some oxen which had strayed the night before. Private William Batty, Co. C, 5th Infantry, of the mounted party was killed. As I saw him in his long Buffalo overcoat, I realized how perfectly helpless he must have been against a savage stripped for the fight.

[On] January 5th we came to very fresh Indian sign. Their camps extended for miles in the valley of Tongue River. Every grove of timber had its war-houses and vast quantities of cotton wood had been stripped of its bark by the ponies. On the 6th, abandoned ponies were met with. We were approaching the Wolf Mountains. [On] January 7th the thermometer dropped to zero, three inches of snow fell the previous night, and we could only make 2½ miles on account of trouble and delay in fording Tongue River. After reaching camp, the scouts surrounded and captured 4 squaws and 4 pappooses further up the valley. Upon returning to see if any bucks were following, they were surrounded and had a hard fight. Their horses were killed, but they were saved by the advance of the mounted party and 4 companies of troops.

[On] January 8th at 7 o.c. A.M. a large body of Northern Cheyennes [and Sioux] supposed to be Crazy Horse's band came down the valley of Tongue River and occupied a belt of timber about a mile from our Camp. A portion advanced to a grove of trees about 600 yards off and the pine-covered bluffs on both sides were occupied. Our camp was in a grove of cottonwood at the base of a high bluff, which was occupied by Co. E, 5th Infantry. Three companies were deployed as skirmishers in the valley on our right and three companies sent to take possession of bluffs on our left. The Indians had some long-range guns, Sharp's, Springfields or Remingtons, but were chiefly armed with Winchesters, and apparently had plenty of ammunition. They could fire into camp from three different points. Their lines extended about 12 miles, some of them going to our rear, but the bluffs were so far off in that direction that they did not waste much ammunition in that quarter. The temperature was 14° and it was snowing. Fires were made by the Indians to make up for lack of clothing, while our men stamped their feet to keep warm. During the 5 hours that the fight continued, a number of Indians was seen to fall, and at 12 o.c. N. there was a great commotion among them. Either a prominent man had been struck on our left, or too many warriors were getting wounded. They moved rapidly up the valley, taking their dead and wounded with them. 1st Lieutenant [Robert] McDonald, commanding Co D, 5th Infantry, took a bluff from the Indians and reported considerable blood upon the snow, and evidence of bodies having been dragged off. Corporal Augustus Rothman, Co. A, 5th Infantry, was shot through the head and instantly killed. Private Henry Rodenburgh, Co. A, 5th Inf, was shot through the face, Private George Danha, Co. H, 5th Infantry, attached to Co. A, received a flesh wound in the breast. Private Bernard McCann, Co. F, 22nd Infantry, received a gunshot fracture of the right femur, in the upper third, and died 4 days afterwards. Several other men received slight wounds which did not interfere with their duties. Capt. [Edmond] Butler, 5th Infantry, had his horse shot under him. One 12-pounder brass piece, and a 3-inch rifle gun, were used, but the guns, which shoot twice, did not appear to demoralize the Indians much. In the afternoon the camp was removed from the valley to the bluff, and in the evening, when the camp fires could be seen, a parting volley was sent at us by their rear-guard. The fires were put out and we rested quietly till morning.

[On] January 9th the weather moderated and rain alternated with snow. At 2 o.c. P.M. Genl Miles with the mounted party, scouts and six companies of troops, went three miles up the valley to see what had become of the Indians. They had withdrawn. The troops returned before dark. [On] January 10th the command started for the Cantonment, distant 110 miles, and arrived on the 18th inst.

Tongue River winds from bluff to bluff, and has to be crossed frequently. One day it was crossed 13 times. It was crossed about 50 times on the march out and about 75 times in returning. Sometimes the stream was free from ice. More frequently it was frozen so solidly that there was little delay in crossing. Again, wagons would break through the ice, upset, and a whole company would have wet feet in getting a wagon out. The oxen were of the greatest service in helping out teams which were hopelessly stalled. The thermometer ranged from $-28°$ on the night of January 11th to 44° on the morning of January 14th. About 50 cases of frostbite occurred on the trip, chiefly toes and heels. The snow ranged from 6 inches to 18 inches in depth, except in the drifts where it was occasionally hip deep. [On] January 4th nearly all the snow melted and next day the men marched through mud. On the 5th it snowed again, and on the 7th the thermometer was at zero.

The majority of the men got their feet wet nearly every day, and those who had to go on picket, upon arriving at camp, had little opportunity to dry their feet. The men provided with Arctic-shoes [rubberized] had scarcely a case of frostbite among them. Those who wore government [leather] shoes and boots suffered most, and some cases occurred among those who wore buffalo overshoes. A few had oiled tanned snow packs which were very well liked. The cable screwed [government issue] shoes would have a deposit of frost around each piece of metal on the inside of the sole every cold morning; many of the boots and shoes would be coated with a cake of ice inside when they were not dried out in the night. It was surprising to see the number of men whose clothes were scorched and burned in their efforts to dry them and get warm. Shoes, pantaloon legs, and coat-skirts were burned in at least 20 per cent of the command. The supplies in the Q.M. Dept not being sufficient, the men had gone heavily in debt to the Post Traders for overalls, socks, Arctic-shoes, gloves, mittens and underclothing. Some men had suits made out of blankets and they were comparatively comfortable. The men have learned to protect their faces very well. Nearly all wore caps with large ear-flaps, and some had a face cover, which only had openings for the eyes and mouth, for the severest weather. Only one man had his face frost-bitten. Not many fingers, and I am glad to be able to say that no toes, will be lost.

The problem to be solved is protection from the cold without being so bundled up as to be helpless. It was the utmost importance in my own case to guard against cold on account of the risk of Dysentry. I succeeded, but I was comparatively helpless. I wore two pair of woolen socks, buffalo mocassins and leggins, and buffalo over-shoes, 2 pr drawers, one of them buck-skin, 2 pr pants, one made out of a blanket, 5 shirts, one of them buckskin and one made out of a blanket, a coat and buffalo overcoat, blanket cap, which would cover the face when necessary, a comforter, buck-skin gloves inside of blanket-lined buck-skin mittens, and yet on two days when marching in the face of a snow and wind storm, I felt as if there were no blood in my body. The men got accustomed to the symptoms of frost-bite and occasionally one could be seen to drop out of the ranks, take off his shoes and rub his toes with snow. As I was riding along one day in the face of a snow and wind storm, with the thermometer down below zero, I saw a man who was rubbing his nose with snow and relieving his mind at the same time by uttering in the most bitter tone, "G——d D——n it." "What's the matter, nipped your nose?" I inquired. "Yes, my nose and fingers and everything else, G——d D——n it." The tone of voice spoke volumes.

The buffalo overcoats are too heavy and long in the skirt for any other use than to protect men on guard. It is extremely difficult to march in them. It would be an improvement to shorten the skirt for field service. The men generally wore leggins made out of shelter-tents, and when these are blanket-lined they are very comfortable and of great service. Blanket underclothing or blanket pants and coats would add greatly to the comfort and efficiency of the men. Duck overalls were worn by many and added much to the comfort of the wearer. Arctics were pronounced by every one to be the most comfortable foot covering to march through snow. It was painful to see men laboring along in buffalo overshoes, the soles of which becoming slippery, they slid all over the surface and gave the men a tumble at nearly every gully and ravine.

One of the minor annoyances to a mounted man is the stirrup in ordinary use. It is too narrow and shallow for buffalo overshoes. In mounting, a small quantity of snow adheres to the sole of the shoe. This is soon converted into a cake of ice in the stirrup, which causes the foot to be constantly slipping out. A broad deep stirrup, such as is used in California and the "Far West" generally obviates this, and saves mental wear and tear immensely.

Fortunately on this expedition there was an abundance of wood and every tent had a roaring fire in front of it. But that does not give much warmth to the tent. Some nights it was impossible for the men to sleep on account of the cold; coughing could be heard from one end of the Battalion to the other, but no serious cases occurred. Cases of Rheumatism from cold, fatigue, and exposure were frequent. If Sibley tents and stoves were used for winter campaigning, it would prevent an immense amount of suffering among the men.

Captain Butler's account of the Battle of Wolf Mountains appeared in the Army and Navy Journal, *March 31, 1877.*

On 29th December Gen. Miles moved from the Cantonment up the valley of the Tongue with Co. A ([Captain James S.] Casey's), Co. C ([Captain Edmond] Butler's), Co. E ([Captain Ezra P.] Ewer's [Ewers's]), of the 5th Infantry, the mounted detachment under Capt. [Lieutenant Charles E.] Hargous, and a three-inch gun under Lieut. [James W.] Pope. [Companies E and F, Twenty-second Infantry, and D, Fifth Infantry, had left earlier, on December 27.] The snow was from six to ten inches deep. The thermometer read 28 deg. below 0 at daybreak, and when the command started was from 10 deg. to 15 deg. below. A slight but bitter wind drove a light, dry, stinging snow in the faces of the men. On the morning of the 31st this force overtook the detachment with the ox-teams, and that night the whole went into camp together.

On New Year's day, 1877, officers and men had an early opportunity of exchanging the compliments of the season. Reveille was at 4.30 A.M., and the march, by moonlight, over the frozen snow. New Year's greetings were short, and sharp as the air they were breathed in. If the air was cold, however, the trail was rather the reverse. About sunset, as the command was moving into a piece of woods, it surprised about twenty-five or thirty Indians. These took to their ponies' heels on being attacked by the Crow scouts, who were in the advance. Here the ox wagons were aban-

Captain Edmond Butler, Fifth U.S. Infantry. Courtesy of Mary Casey.

doned. The oxen were driven along. On a pinch, tough beef is better than no rations. On the 3d, Private William H. Batlin [Batty], of Co. C, 5th Infantry, attached to the mounted detachment, while acting as a flanker on the right rear, was killed by a party of twenty-five Indians suddenly dashing out of a ravine. They had no time to mutilate him, however. One of the oxen was wounded by an arrow at the same time.

On 5th January, Indian signs grew thicker and thicker. More cattle were picked up and remains of recently slaughtered oxen were found. Miles of hastily abandoned war lodges were passed. The country became very rough. The valley of the Tongue grew narrower, the stream more tortuous, and the hills on both sides loftier and more precipitous, until the valley shrank into a prolonged and winding canon. At short distances, jutting bluffs made narrow passes which offered points of vantage to the savage enemy. The gorges of the Wolf Mountains had been reached. It began thawing. Animals broke through the ice and men got wet extricating them. It was not an uncommon sight, that of a soldier sitting in the snow and rubbing with it a naked foot that was as white and looked cold and marble-like as the foot of a statue.

On the 6th, the march was through a large war camp, recently and hurriedly abandoned. Unusual heat was followed by snow. In the evening there was snow and hail driven by a cruel wind, and by 5 P.M. it was pitch dark. On the evening of the 7th the scouts captured four Cheyenne squaws, a youth about fourteen years, and three younger children. Two hundred to two hundred and fifty Indians made a dash at the scouts, shot two of their horses and made a desperate effort to take them, but Major Casey, with Co. A, 5th Infantry, the mounted party under Capt. Hargous and a gun, was sent to the relief of the scouts. Casey opened a musketry on the Indians, and darkness supervening, they withdrew.

Next morning, Jan. 8th, the fight renewed shortly after daylight. [Lieutenant Mason] Carter's Co. (K), 5th Infantry, [Captain Charles J.] Dickey's company and [Lieutenant Cornelius C.] Cusick's of the 22nd, were deployed across the valley—the first mentioned to the west of Tongue River—the other two to the east of that stream, all fronting to the south, the left resting at the base of a bluff under which the train was parked. This bluff formed the slope of the first plateau of the Wolf Range. Casey's company was deployed along the front edge of this plateau, supporting the 3-inch gun. To the left of the gun, on a conical knoll which rose abruptly from the edge of the plateau, Capt. Ewer's [sic] Co. (E), was posted. Capt. Butler, 5th Infantry, with a division composed of his own company (C), and [Lieutenant Robert] McDonald's (D), held the rear of the position in the valley, facing northward, where the Tongue bends across the valley from west to east.

The Indians charged down the valley in large force, close up to the skirmish line, and wounded two of the animals in the pack train. They failed to make an impression, however. Then they turned their attention to the flanks. They began to swarm on the bluffs to the right. Some were already occupying a bluff to the left and slightly to the rear of the knoll held by Capt. Ewers. It commanded Capt. Ewers' position. Gen. Miles ordered Casey to occupy this bluff, and brought up Butler with his company from the valley to take the position hitherto occupied by Casey. Soon after he ordered up McDonald with Co. D, and put him in on Butler's right. The hill Casey had to take was high and steep, and flattened on the top. While crossing the intervening plain, Casey was met by a heavy fire from the hills to the right of that he was ordered to take. With considerable difficulty, on account of the snow and ice and loose stones, and the precipitous character of the hill, Casey succeeded in taking it. When he had reached the summit, a party of Indians, dismounted, advanced on a

The Battle of Wolf Mountains, January 8, 1877. From *Frank Leslie's Illustrated*

neck between him and another hill, situated to his left front, and charged him, but were repulsed with loss. The Chief Medicine Man—Ka-hi-ton-ka, or Big Crow—and one of the head warriors, nephew of one of the captive squaws, were killed here. Soon, fire was opened on Casey from a high hill to his left. Gen. Miles sent McDonald with Co. D to drive the enemy from this position, which he did. The action then became general. The Indians tried every point of the line. They were in strong force. The hills and woods resounded with their cries and the high pitched voices of the chiefs giving their orders and trying to "fire the Indian heart."

After a time the demonstrations in the valley became less energetic. The Indians disappeared from the bluffs on the right, and, crossing the bed of the stream, were massing in the pines on the principal spur of the main ridge, preparing some move to drive Casey and McDonald from their positions, which were commanded by this, the dominant point of the field. This spur was to the left of McDonald, separated from him by a ravine, and took the whole line on reverse. The Indians to the number of 200 to 250 were massing on this lofty ridge. Quick as thought Gen. Miles threw Butler's Co. (C) against them. Butler led off his company by the left, taking the double time, and deploying it by that flank in skirmisher order as it moved. The Indians met this movement with a continuous and heavy fire on this company as it crossed the plain toward the base of the ridge, a distance of a quarter of a mile. Lieut. Baldwin, A.A.A.G., rode down the line cheering on the men. Facing by the right flank, the company charged up the first rise. The left of the company was a little in advance, owing to the nature of the initial movement. From ravines, and from behind rocks and fallen trees, the force was concentrated on this portion of the line. It seemed to those who watched the movement that nothing could save this company from decimation. Butler's horse

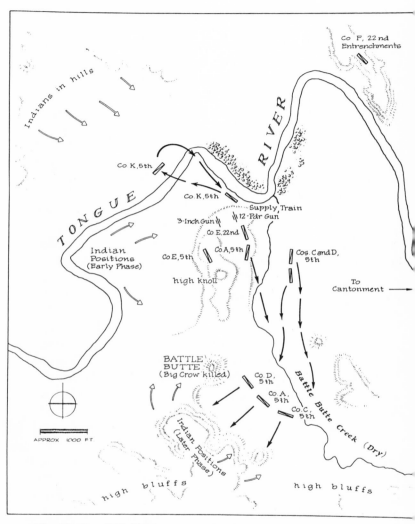

The Battle of Wolf Mountains, January 8, 1877.

was shot under him as he led the charge up the first ascent. The steepest part of the ridge was yet to be scaled. Giving the Indians in the ravine a volley, and taking the run, Co. C moved up, its commander now on foot. The men behaved admirably, dashed up through the snow and over rocks, firing as they advanced—not a man of the company or the detachments of G and F attached to it, lagging or flinching—and drove the Indians from the hill. Many of these were concealed behind fallen cedars and improvised breastworks of flat stones. From these positions they fired volley after volley. Fully 400 shots were fired at this company from Winchester and Sharps rifles, and, under Providence, only the plunging nature of the fire, which made it too high, the precipate rapidity with which the Indians worked their magazine guns, which made it uncertain, and the impetuous rush of the men which demoralized their opponents, saved this company from heavy loss. As the Indians retreated, snow began to fall, and the height was crowned in a snow storm.

By this move Gen. Miles decided the struggle. This ridge was the key-point of the position. It took the main line on reverse and flanked and commanded the hills taken by Casey and McDonald. It was a pretty move, conceived and ordered on the same moment, and that the right one. Had the company been repulsed, the Indians would have gained so much confidence that not three companies could have taken it.

The force at Gen. Miles' command was about 400 men. The number put in line of battle was about 300. Officers were scarce. No company had more than one officer for duty with it. The Indian fighting force was about 600 warriors, Cheyennes and Ogallallas, at the very lowest estimate. They were principally armed with Winchester rifles. For people who were supposed to be short of ammunition, they used it rather lavishly. They expended as much as, nay, more than, the troops. They had chosen their ground.

It has since been learned that they expected to make another Custer slaughter. The Cheyenne captives, in the hands of the troops, sang songs of triumph during the entire fight, in anticipation of a speedy rescue and the savage orgies of a massacre. Nor was Crazy Horse, the Indian leader, that day, an adversary to be despised. He tried every point of our lines, but the quick and wary leader pitted against him, anticipated every move and foiled and punished each successive attempt. It is now known that this was Crazy Horse's first fight since the Custer massacre, and the first time he has been defeated and driven from the field [*sic*].

The loss of the troops in this expedition was three killed—two men of the 5th Infantry and one of the 22d—and eight wounded. Three horses were killed, one horse and two mules wounded. Eleven Indians, including the "Big Medicine Man," Ka-hi-ton-ka, and the war chief, were killed in front of Casey's company. The Indians got the body of the war chief, which they carried away on a travois, with great manifestations of grief, but they had to leave the body of the Medicine chief. Two saddles were emptied by Butler's men as they charged the hill, and five by McDonald's. In front of the latter companies numerous stains of blood were found on the snow among the pines and cedars. Five were killed by the scouts and others in the valley, which for miles further up showed tracks of blood in the snow on the scattering trails of the flying enemy.

While the heaviest work of the day fell to the companies of Casey, Butler and McDonald, those in the valley were not idle. They were engaged all the morning, and determined efforts were made by the Indians to drive back the centre before they tried the turning moves by the left. It is the opinion of some who had had years of experience in Indian fighting, that there has rarely, if ever, been a fight before in which the Sioux and Cheyennes showed such determination and persistency, where they were finally defeated. They were evidently promised a massacre, but "the medicine was not good," and the poor Medicine Man could not even heal himself. They came close enough to shoot the pack animals in the park. There, under fire, Drs. Tilton and Tesson attended to the wounded. The former officer went out to the bluff taken by Major Casey to attend the wounded there.

Lieut. J. W. Pope, 5th Infantry, assisted by Lieut. E. W. Casey of the 22d, did good and effective work in shelling out ravines and dense pieces of woods with a 3-inch gun and a brass 12-pounder. Lieut. H. K. Baily was A.A.Q.M., and Lieut. O. F. Long, acting engineer officer of the expedition.

Crazy Horse was driven out of the Tongue valley and the Wolf Mountains, and is now with a portion of his followers seeking another and more secure winter camp in the Big Horn Mountains.

For several days the troops had to march through snow two or three feet deep. The thaw made the ice on Tongue River treacherous, and mules and wagons had frequently to be taken out by sheer force when they broke through it. The river had to be crossed 150 times. There were several cases of frost bite, but none that will result in permanent injury. The men were as well protected as was possible, under the circumstances, by caps, leggings, overalls, and blanket-shirts of their own manufacture. They showed in a high degree the best qualities of a soldier. But the man who worked hardest, longest and most unceasingly—whose last thought seemed to be comfort or rest for himself—was the officer in command, Gen. Miles.

Chapter 15
The Lame Deer Fight, May 7, 1877
John F. McBlain

Miles's victory at Wolf Mountains triggered massive surrenders of the Sioux and Cheyennes. The majority turned themselves in over the next several months at the Red Cloud and Spotted Tail agencies in northwestern Nebraska. Crazy Horse surrendered in May 1877. Other tribesmen went to the Cheyenne River and Standing Rock agencies along the Missouri River in Dakota Territory. Still other warriors and their families trailed in to the Tongue River cantonment and surrendered to Miles. Sitting Bull and his few hundred followers journeyed beyond the international border into Canada, where, for the most part, they remained as refugees until 1881, when they traveled south to Fort Buford on the Missouri and surrendered as prisoners of war.

In May 1877, as the various surrenders proceeded, one group of Minneconjou Sioux under Lame Deer announced intentions to defy the government and to continue hunting in the Powder River country. Miles immediately set out after this band, which was camped on a tributary of the Rosebud called Muddy Creek. The Lame Deer Fight of May 7, 1877 (also known as the Muddy Creek Fight), constituted the last major action in the Great Sioux War and was Miles's last victory in the conflict.

John F. McBlain, who wrote the following narrative of the pursuit and fight with Lame Deer's people, was a sergeant of Company L, Second Cavalry, when he participated in these events. A Pennsylvanian, McBlain joined the army in 1872 and served in an enlisted capacity with the regiment until 1880, when he was commissioned second lieutenant in the Ninth Cavalry. He was promoted to first lieutenant in 1887 and to captain in 1897. McBlain was still in the service at the time of his death in 1902. His account of the Muddy Creek fight was published in the Journal of the United States Cavalry Association *10 (June 1897).*

THE WINTER OF 1876, following the Custer massacre, witnessed unusual military activity on the Yellowstone. General N. A. Miles, then colonel of the Fifth Infantry, was placed in command of the forces left in that section of country when the greater part of the troops that had been busy during the summer campaign were withdrawn for the winter.

General Miles's command consisted of his own regiment and part of the Twenty-second Infantry, under Major [Lieutenant Colonel] Elwell S. Otis. The hostile Sioux that had broken up into numerous small bands and scattered all over the country immediately after the Little Big Horn fight, and had by reason of doing so eluded the vigorous pursuit made by Generals Terry and Crook, had a merry time of it in keeping out of the way of General Miles, who chased and followed them back and forth across the Yellowstone about a dozen times, keeping them constantly on the move, giving them no rest until they found it to their advantage to go into the agencies and live off the bountiful provision made for them by our merciful and forgiving government.

Aside from those hostiles that had crossed the line into British territory, the only ones known to be out was a small camp of about three hundred, made up of the discontented of nearly all the hostile tribes.

To drive in or to catch and punish this band, General Miles organized a campaign in the spring of 1877. The troops engaged in this duty were four troops of the Second Cavalry, being the same squadron that Custer declined to take with him on his march up the Rosebud to his death the summer before, believing his own twelve troops strong enough, four companies of the Twenty-second Infantry and one company of the Fifth Infantry as train guard.

On May 1st the command left the Cantonment at the mouth of Tongue River and marched up that river until on the 4th, about noon, the column was halted and preparations were made for dinner. Just about the time it was prepared orders were passed along to hurry and get the packs ready; we were going to leave the wagons, as information had been brought in by the scouts that precluded the possibility of taking wheels. It didn't take us long to get the "packs" ready, as they were to carry nothing but ammunition and rations.

The march was resumed across to the Rosebud, almost at right angles to the direction in which we had been marching. We crossed the Rosebud a little before sunset and continued the march all night, and the sun of the next day was well up in the heavens before we halted for a short rest and breakfast.

During the night we had passed over quite a raise in the hills west of the Rosebud, known by the Indians as "The Big Hill." At times it seemed that we could hear the rushing of water a long distance below us, and that a misstep by a horse would hurry his rider into the unknown. This hill was crossed at night as a precaution against being seen by any of the hostiles that might be out hunting in the hills.

The command was guided by half-breed "Johnny" Brourier [Bruguier] and "Hump," a Cheyenne [Sioux] warrior; they knew their business and were determined to keep their promise to General Miles, to place his command on top of the hostile camp without the Indians knowing it.

All day May 5th we marched through the hills west of the Rosebud, passing camp after camp of the hostiles. Many of them presented evidences of having been recently occupied, these evidences being fresher with each succeeding camp. May 6th was nearly all spent the same way; we knew that we were getting closer and closer to our quarry; it didn't need the warnings and assurances of our scouts to enlighten us; the deserted camps spoke only too plainly of our proximity to the hostiles.

The camps gave no signs of hurried departure, which

fact bespoke either an ignorance on the part of the enemy of our near presence or a confidence and willingness to meet us, when and where they thought best. We felt satisfied that our nearness was unknown to them even if they were aware of troops being out after them.

About 2 o'clock on the afternoon of the 6th the column was halted, messages were sent to the subordinate commanders which soon caused them to gather with the General at the head of the column. In a short time orders were given for the cavalry to take two days rations in their saddle pockets, and each troop to take one pack mule with two thousand rounds of ammunition, the infantry to remain with the pack train and follow the trail of the cavalry as speedily as prudent.

The cavalry cut loose from the infantry at a good stiff jog, keeping it up until about 8 o'clock, when it went into bivouac in a "pocket"; strict and positive orders were given against striking matches or making a light of any kind.

The General called his officers together and informed them that the hostile camp had been definitely located and that he intended to "jump" it at daybreak next morning; to do this it would be necessary for the troops to be in the saddle about midnight, and directions were given to that effect; the plan of the coming fight was outlined and dispositions made, contingent upon the Indians standing and fighting. At midnight the command was quickly and quietly aroused, each and every man keenly alive to the importance of making no noise that might be carried on the midnight air to the enemy and give the alarm.

It needed but a few minutes for the troops that had been campaigning in the Sioux country for several years past to get into shape and form column. As soon as everything had been reported up, the column started at a good sharp trot and kept it up for about twenty miles, when we swung down out of the hills into the valley of the Rosebud. It was one of the most exhilarating experiences I ever had;

all nature seemed awake and appeared to have put on newer and fresher charms to greet us and speed us on our way.

It was not until we were about to turn into the valley of Muddy Creek that rein was drawn; the hostile camp was then but a few miles ahead of us. To be ready for any emergency a brief halt was made to adjust saddles and tighten girths. Troop "H," Lieutenant L. H. Jerome commanding, was in advance, and was told off to take the herd; in this he was to be assisted by Lieutenant Ed. Casey, Twenty-second Infantry. Troops "F," Captain [George] Tyler, and "G," Captain [James N.] Wheelan, were to compose the fighting line, while Troop "L," Captain [Randolph] Norwood, was in support.

How we did go galloping up that valley, now troop front, now in column of fours, the changes in formation made necessary by the windings of the stream. The camp was struck at about 4 o'clock on the morning of May 7th, every man in the command seemed to partake of the spirit of the General in whom they had so much confidence, and felt that upon the result of this fight depended whether or not the Sioux would remain "good."

The hostiles disappointed General Miles somewhat, as they did not wait to fight for their "homes and firesides" but took to the hills. The General was equal to the change of conditions; he quickly turned the leading troop (Tyler's) up a "draw" to the right, pushed the next troop (Wheelan's) through the village to a corresponding position on the other side of a hill facing the village; Norwood's troop was quickly deployed, dismounted and advanced through the village and up the hill. Upon this hill the Indians had massed and Norwood would never have gotten up if Tyler had not first been in position to get in a cross fire and thus occupy the attention of at least a part of the Indians; the hill was so steep that it was as much as the men could do to creep up it without having to fight at the same time.

As soon as the camp had been attacked General Miles had it made known to the hostiles that they could surrender and be properly taken care of. Lame Deer and Iron Star, the two head men of the camp, seemed desirous of taking advantage of this offer, and approached to within a few yards of General Miles. Lame Deer placed his gun on the ground as an earnest of his good intentions, and Iron Star seemed about to follow his example, when one of the citizen scouts near the General fired at the Indian; immediately Iron Star fired at the group with the General, and Lame Deer, grasping his gun, stepped back about five yards, and taking deliberate aim fired directly at the General. How the bullet missed the one it was fired at is one of those mysterious things that happen in all battles. The Indian was not more than ten yards from General Miles when he fired, and the bullet hit a soldier [Private Charles Shrenger] of "H" Troop, who was in line with the General, behind him, in the breast, killing him instantly.

The audacity of the move and the suddenness with which it took place, coupled with concern for the General's welfare, so occupied the attention of those with the General, that the two chiefs made good their retreat to the hills, only to die there. Although "F" Troop was pouring into them a heavy fire, the Indians fought stubbornly, and it was no easy task for "L" troop to get a foothold on the hill, but it succeeded in doing so, and Lame Deer was killed within a few minutes thereafter. Iron Star saw that his comrade had received his death wound and tried, in the face of a hot and continuous fire, to drag him away, but the troops were pressing them too closely, and he was obliged to abandon his friend, though he did it reluctantly. The trend of the hills was off in the direction of where "G" Troop was, and as the Indians followed them, they were brought right under the fire of that troop, and Iron Star was killed there, within thirty yards of the place he had to leave his chief.

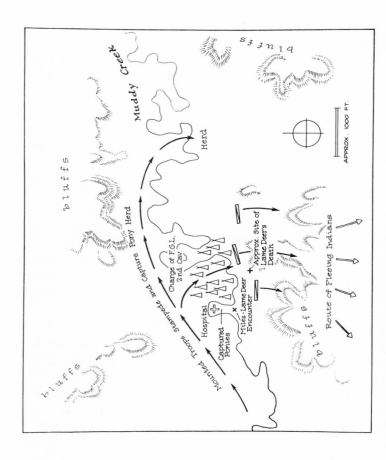

The Lame Deer Fight, May 7, 1877.

From that time until the hostiles finally got down into the valley of the Rosebud, the fight was a running one, the Indians making stands at every place presenting good opportunities of checking the advance of the troops, to cover the retreat of their families.

Jerome and Casey "jumped" the herd and captured it. The boys whose province it was to put the horses out to graze had just done so and were returning to camp, when the troops were upon them. Had we been ten minutes earlier or ten minutes later in attacking the camp, we would not have been so successful in getting the herd; as it was, the Indians got away with not more than a dozen horses. The captured herd consisted of about 600 head of fine horses, and were used to mount the Fifth Infantry.

The infantry reached us about noon.

Many times during the day a few Indians would appear upon some one of the many hills around the camp, and after firing a couple of volleys into us, would scamper off. Fortunately, there was but one of these volleys that did any harm. A soldier of "H" Troop was engaged in frying some meat, having his frying pan over the fire, when a bullet shattered his arm, making him drop his pan, which he did with the exclamation: "D——n it, there goes my bacon."

During the night the camp was protected by a chain of sentinels entirely encircling it, and an almost incessant firing was kept up from dark to daylight, which had its influence in deterring the Indians from making a break through the camp to stampede the herd, for it is very probable that had they found a part of the line not responsive to their challenge of fire, that part would have been visited in force.

The valley was narrow, with high commanding hills on either side. The Indians in numbers were covering those behind us, watching our every movement, and it required good judgment to get the command out of the valley down into the broader one of the Rosebud, with the large herd of captured horses, without serious trouble, and it had to be done by "backing out." The Indians were ready to take advantage of mistakes and to pounce upon us, but the opportunity longed for did not present itself.

This was the last of the fights in that long series incident to the Sioux War. The defeat of the Indians was most complete. Everything they owned, aside from what little they had on, was abandoned in the wild rush for the hills when they heard the near approach of the troops. It removed forever from their minds the erroneous impression that they were superior fighters to the troops. Their entire camp was destroyed, together with large stores of dried meat, and all at the expense of four soldiers killed and one officer and five soldiers wounded.

Index

Teton Sioux Indians. *See* Sioux Indians
Texas, 96, 167, 168, 187
Third Cavalry, 8, 13, 15, 17, 97, 102; in Rosebud
    Creek battle, 28, 31–33, 36, 37; in skirmish at
    Tongue River, 24; in Slim Buttes battle,
    102–103, 113–15
Tilton, Henry R., 203; biographical data on, 186–87
Tongue River, 20–22, 25, 27, 39, 63, 65–67, 73, 99,
    116, 117, 120, 156, 167, 174, 189, 191, 196, 197,
    203, 205
Tongue River, skirmish at, 22–24; casualties, 24;
    map, 21
Tongue River Cantonment, 126, 134, 145, 162, 166,
    186, 187, 189, 191, 194, 204, 205
Tongue River Valley, 186, 188–90, 194, 203
Twenty-second Infantry, 92, 116; in expedition
    against Minneconjous and Lame Deer fight,
    205–11; in Spring Creek encounters, 117–31; in
    Wolf Mountains expedition and battle, 187,
    190–94, 197–202
Tyler, George, 208

U.S. Military Academy, 132
University of Pennsylvania, 186
Utah ("Mormon") War, 134
Ute Indians (scouts), 97

Van Vliet, Frederick, 37, 38
Varnum, Charles A., 44, 45, 47, 61
Von Luettwitz, Adolphus H., 110, 114
Vroom, Peter D., 32

Walker, George B., 92
Warbonnet Creek, 79, 83, 85
Warbonnet Creek, Skirmish at, 85–91; map of, 86
War Department, 3, 182
Washakie, 24
West Point, N.Y., 70, 79, 96, 116
Wheelan, James, 208